Contents

the 1984 SCOUT annual

The Official Cub Scout Annual of The Scout Association
Edited by David Harwood

The Cover Photograph

Cub Scout Hedley Myers stands in the cockpit of his father's Hawk aircraft at RAF Kemble, home of the Red Arrows until this year. You can see and read about what happened when three Cub Scouts (including Hedley) were guests of the Red Arrows on page 9.
Photograph by Andy Carnall

This Annual belongs to:

£ 2.95

INDOOR OBSTACLE COURSE

devised and drawn by Vic Clapham

4 CLIMB THROUGH BOTTOMLESS CORRUGATED CARDBOARD BOXES.
5 RUN IN A SACK.
6 STEP INTO SPACED CARDBOARD BOXES.
14 EAT MARSHMALLOW FISH... NO HANDS!
13 TIE A REEF KNOT.
FINISH

Cliff Brown's Puzzle Page . . .

FOR THIS YEAR'S ANNUAL, CLIFF BROWN HAS DEVISED FOUR PUZZLE PAGES FOR YOU TO SOLVE. HERE'S THE FIRST ONE— YOU'LL FIND THE OTHERS ON PAGES—24—42—57.

OBSTACLE COURSE MAZE

THIS CUB SCOUT LEADER HAS THOUGHT UP A SCHEME TO REALLY TEST THE STAMINA OF THESE THREE BOYS IN HIS PACK. FIRST THEY MUST CLIMB THE TREE BY FINDING A ROUTE WHICH WILL MAKE AN **UNBROKEN LINE** FROM THE FEET OF THE CUB ON THE LEFT (WHICH WE'VE MARKED WITH AN 'X') INTO THE TOP OF THE OLD CASTLE TOWER. NEXT THEY HAVE TO GET DOWN FROM THE TOP OF THE TOWER TO THE DOORWAY **WITHOUT CROSSING A BLACK LINE**. FINALLY THEY MUST RETURN THROUGH THE UNDERGROWTH BY FINDING ANOTHER **UNBROKEN LINE** BACK TO THE POINT FROM WHICH THEY STARTED.

FIND THE CUB SCOUT PROMISE

CAREFULLY STUDY THE LETTER GRID BELOW. ALL THE WORDS OF THE CUB SCOUT PROMISE ARE IN IT. EACH WORD WILL BE FOUND SPELT OUT BACKWARDS OR FORWARDS, AND HORIZONTALLY, VERTICALLY OR DIAGONALLY. EACH TIME YOU FIND A WORD, CAREFULLY RING IT ROUND ON THE GRID AND MARK IT OFF THE PROMISE. (BY THE WAY, MANY OF THE WORDS OVERLAP EACH OTHER—WE DID NOT WANT TO MAKE IT TOO EASY!)

M	E	C	O	V	P	B	D	B	C	K
R	D	N	A	N	E	E	U	Q	O	D
I	T	U	X	S	S	C	O	U	T	O
T	H	A	T	I	M	U	T	P	I	P
H	E	D	M	Y	Q	T	H	E	L	E
E	V	O	T	H	E	R	D	N	A	E
L	R	G	O	T	O	L	L	I	W	K
P	O	B	Y	T	A	C	K	M	G	D

A Musical Secret Code

by N. R. Miles

As a Cub Scout it's not necessary to tell you about the fun you can have with secret codes, but have you ever thought of using musical notes to send a message?

Normally the notes are identified by the letters A to G as you can see on this diagram. Can you de-code the words which are "hidden" in the five musical bars? (The answers are given upside down at the bottom of the page.)

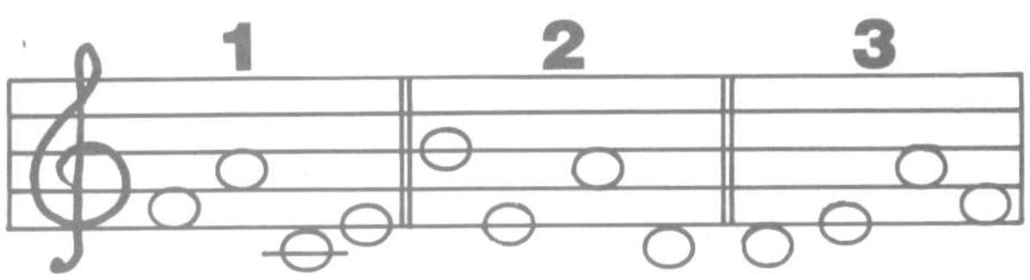

If you want to improvise and add letters choose a code word and add the extra letters to the music. Here is an example.
The code word is SOUTH. The notes are as follows:

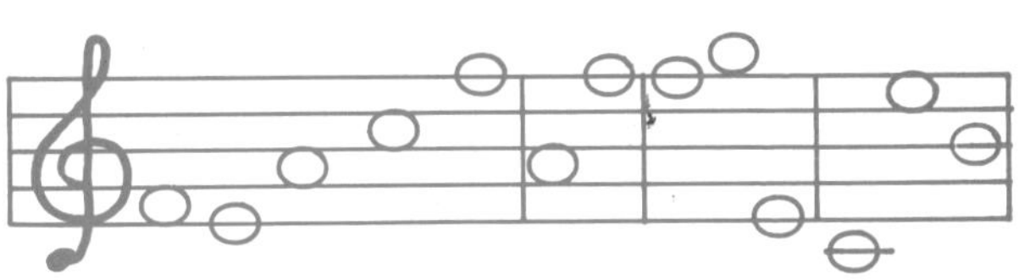

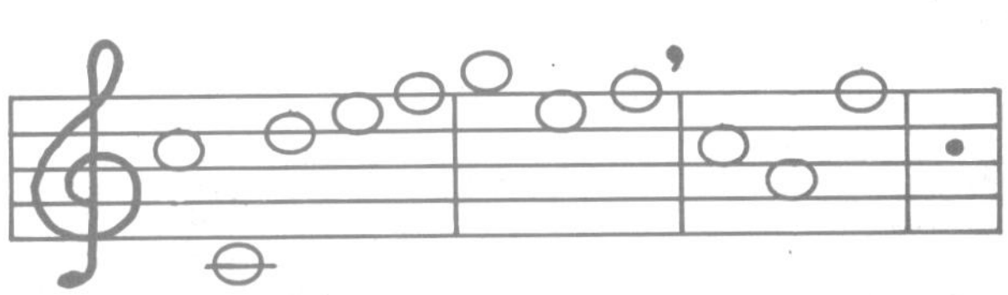

Of course, you still have not got a complete alphabet. You could make one up by using sharps and flats to denote other letters.

ANSWERS

1. FACE 2. BEAD 3. DEAF 4. FADED 5. BADGE

A SCOUTING CROSSWORD

by Suzanne Brown

Clues Across:

1. At the age of nineteen Baden-Powell was made a sub-lieutenant in the 13th ------- (7)
6. In 1909 Baden-Powell was made a ------ (6)
7. --- Scouts are interested in aeronautical subjects (3)
9. These games are played outside (4)
10. A Cub Scout works for his ----- Badges (5)
11. When Baden-Powell left school he joined the ---- (4)
13. "Be prepared" is the Scout ----- (5)
14. A team race (5)
15. The Scout ---- is made when any Member of the Scout Movement makes his Promise (4)

Clues Down:

1. There is a ---- on the First Aider Proficiency Badge (4)
2. Found on the Explorer Proficiency Badge (8)
3. A Cub Scout may work for his ---ist Proficiency Badge (3)
4. A Scout works for the Scout -------- (8)
5. A Cub Scout learns to treat ----s and scalds when working for his Gold Arrow (4)
8. Found on the Handyman Badge (6)
12. A short story (4)

Solution on page 63

IT'S A CUB'S LIFE!

Illustrated by Leslie Cecil

In the 1982 CUB SCOUT ANNUAL we asked you to write and tell us what it was like to be a Cub. We wanted you to let us know about a particular project, event, incident or activity which you had enjoyed as a Cub. Lots of you did. It was a difficult job choosing the best – but here they are. The writer of each of these items has received £2 and a free copy of this Annual. As well as our main competition, there's another 'challenge' this year – the details are on page 41.

Filthy!

One Monday I went to Cubs and I was really smart because some younger boys were being Invested. When I got there I became filthy because I rolled all over the floor and played football like I always do.
CHRISTOPHER JONES,
4th Teignmouth, Devon.

Up all night

I like Cubs because it's fun and joyful. When we went to camp with the Pack we were up all night because all the Pack were telling jokes. My auntie bought me the 1982 Annual because she knew I was a Cub, and I would like to win a 1984 Annual.
MICHAEL WADE,
5th Newham, East Ham, London.

Exhausted

It was great fun going to Brownsea Island for the day. We went there by boat with lots of other schools. It was a long, steep walk and we were exhausted when we got to the top, but it was good fun. We had long explores and our Cub Scout Leader told us about the life of Baden-Powell. After tea we went home.
PHILIP COTTRELL,
Farleigh House Pack, Kent.

Crackers

At Christmas our Group had a fancy dress party. My Mum dressed me up as a Christmas cracker by sewing red crepe paper to a roll of corrugated paper which covered me from head to foot. It was cheap to make, costing

less than £1. I was awarded Third Prize. We also had a Lego building competition with the Pack split into teams and allowed to build a model of their own choice. The winning team built a rocket of considerable size, but most of all we had a terrific time.
STEVEN BERRY,
1st Newport, Isle of Wight.

No tents!

For Cub camp we went to Exeter in a muddy field. Then we sorted ourselves into Sixes. Mine was Navaho because we were doing a project on Indians. But three of the Sixes (including mine) had to stay inside because some of the tents

hadn't arrived. The next day we did some compass work and made a chess board. The following day we went to a Museum and bought things for our families.
JAMES CHINNERY,
5th/7th Wells (Skipper Coats),
Somerset.

Cross country

Myself and all the Cubs went to the cross country. First it was the turn of the under 9s to run. My friend Steven Holloway came 51st. I ran in the over 10½s and came 91st out of 125.
PAUL HUDD,
2nd Patchway (Blenheims), Bristol.

My favourite outing with the Cubs was a visit to Ipswich Town Football Club at Portman Road. We were shown the pitch, the practice pitch, the boot room, the laundry room, the referee's room and the cloakroom. We saw the huge bath the players use after matches, the gym and the place for Cups, which was locked up, but we did see the U.E.F.A. Cup which Ipswich had won. Before we left we saw the Board Room with a lovely crystal light.
CARL HOARE,
Kesgrave, Ipswich, Suffolk.

Screams

It was Cub night. It was a lovely evening. Akela told the younger Cubs we were going stalking while the older ones would stay behind at the hut and practise fire lighting. On the way back Akela asked us to collect thin sticks. We wondered why. Back at the hut the fires were lit. We were to use our

sticks to make dampers. They were delicious, but we suddenly heard screams. We had disturbed a bees' nest and several Cubs and Bagheera had been stung. A delightful evening for me turned out to be a disaster for some.
ADAM MOORE,
Leckhampton, Gloucestershire.

There's more It's a Cub's Life on page 20

A Day with THE RED ARROWS

(above) The Red Arrows' familiar diamond formation.

reporter: David Harwood
photographs: Andy Carnall, Red Arrows Team Photographer

(left) The Coat of Arms of the Red Arrows, officially approved by Her Majesty the Queen.

(below) Kingsley, Hedley and Nicholas with the pilots of the 1982 team.

How many of you have *not* heard of the Red Arrows? Very few, I expect. In fact, I'd guess that those of you who have not seen them 'live' will have watched them on television. You'll have marvelled at the way those nine brightly painted red, white and blue aircraft streak across the sky, seemingly wingtip-to-wingtip, in perfect formation. They bank and roll, twist and turn, loop and break with such precision that it's sometimes hard to believe that each aircraft is being individually flown by a pilot.

But who are the pilots? What are they like? How is their display planned? Where do they practice? THE CUB SCOUT ANNUAL decided to find out. We wrote to the Red Arrows at the Royal Air Force's Central Flying School Detachment, Kemble, near Cirencester in Gloucestershire, and asked if two or three Cub Scouts could spend the day with them.

'I'm sure that we will be able to accommodate you fully in this venture,' came the reply from Flight Lieutenant John Myers, who is one of the pilots. When I asked whether any of the team had sons who were Cub Scouts, John Myers said: 'Yes – me!''

I thought it would be a good idea if our other two Cub Scout investigators also came from the local Pack. After all, the Red Arrows were based in the village. Jackie Hill, the Cub Scout Leader of the Deer Park (Kemble) Cub Scout Pack, arranged for two more boys to come.

And so it was that I met Hedley Myers, Kingsley Gurney and Nicholas Crofts with Jackie Hill at the entrance to RAF Kemble on a warm June day. We reported to the gatehouse and were given a police escort across the airfield to the huge hangars which are the Red Arrows' 'home'. The British Aerospace Hawks were lined up outside.

We went through a door which led us to a long corridor, off which were all sorts of rooms and offices.

'We're quite ordinary people,' Fl. Lt. Myers told the Cubs as he welcomed them. 'We just wear funny red suits!'

He took us to the Crew Room for some refreshments. The walls were lined with trophies, presents, pictures and mementos which had been given to the team by individuals and organisations over the years. Then the boys started to ask questions.

Hedley and Kingsley looking through one of the Red Arrows' Log Books in the Crew Room.

In the Administration Room, Fl. Lt. Myers explained the month-by-month planner on which the details of the programme were given.

How do you join the Red Arrows?

First of all you volunteer. There are always many more volunteers than there are places! We're all serving RAF pilots, so each of us belongs to a particular squadron. Before he can volunteer, a pilot must have completed at least 1,000 hours flying swept wing jet aircraft and have done some formation flying, but he does not have to have flown formation aerobatics, although he will certainly have flown aerobatics in his last squadron.

Does a place become vacant only when someone decides they've had enough?

No. If you're accepted, you are posted from your squadron to serve in the team for three years, so there are usually three 'new' pilots each year.

When did you join the Red Arrows?

In August 1980, so I'll be in the team until the end of the 1983 season.

How long have there been nine aircraft in the team?

Since 1965, when the team first came into existence as the full-time aerobatic team of the Royal Air Force.

The Cubs walked along the corridor, the walls of which were hung with photographs of display teams of the past. They went into the Administration Room. The first thing which caught their eyes was a large month-by-month planner.

This is a very important part of the team's organisation because it's here that the administrative staff and Manager cope with all the details of our programme . . .

But it's only for six months of the year! What do you do for the rest of the time?

Our display season finishes at the end of September. The team then has some leave and our aeroplanes are thoroughly overhauled. After some 'normal' training we come back to start work on the new year's programme. We'll have three new team members, and possibly a new Leader, who may well have some ideas of his own. I'll tell you a bit more about the form of our displays when we go to the Briefing Room. Anyway, the possible formations are worked out on paper and only then do we try them out 'carefully' in the air. We'll practise over Kemble and then in March go out to Cyprus – where we know the weather will be good

Using the magnetic board in the Briefing Room, Fl. Lt. Myers demonstrated how the team changed from one formation to another during a display.

In the Navigation Room, Fl. Lt. Myers showed the Cubs how maps were used to plan a display at a particular location. The map showing the area around RAF Kemble is on the wall behind the boys.

Two of the many pieces of equipment which the Cubs examined in the Safety Equipment Room – a helmet and the test cabinet which tests the helmet's microphone, earphones and oxygen supply connections and systems.

– to put the finishing touches to the whole display.

How many displays do you give in a year?

About 120 – and that's quite a lot! Sometimes we'll give two or three in one day, and we also give displays overseas. Moving our 'circus' about from place-to-place, and looking after the aircraft and men is a big task for the Engineering Officer. We pilots are only the front men for a large, efficient team.

How many people are involved?

There are 80 Royal Air Force technicians under the command of two Engineering Officers. During the display season a completely self-sufficient engineering support team of 25 men travels with us. Nine airmen and the Engineering Officer fly in the rear seats of the Hawks, and the rest usually go in our Hercules. Here at Kemble there are 55 airmen in the Rectification Ground Crew and 5 personnel in administrative support.

The boys went from Administration to the Briefing Room which was set out like a small cinema. They settled in the comfortable chairs as Fl. Lt. Myers went through the sequence of the 1982 formations using aeroplane outlines and a magnetic board.

Most of the work goes on in here. All our practices and displays are video recorded and we watch the playbacks so we can see exactly what we did – right or wrong!

What happens if the weather isn't very good? Do you still give a display?

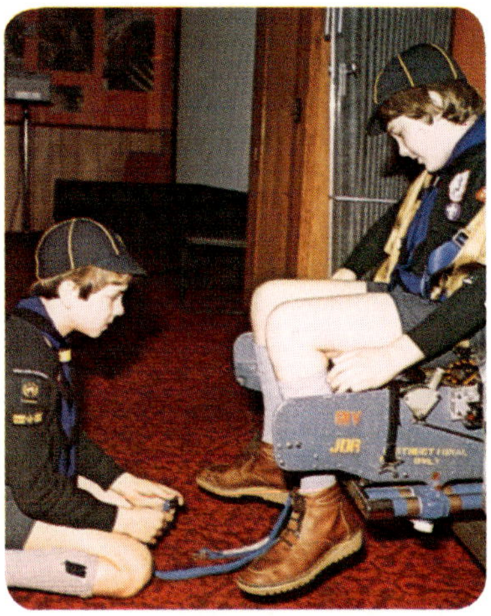

Hedley and Kingsley tried out the demonstration ejector seat.

Ideally we don't want a cloud in the sky. To do our full display, which lasts 15 minutes, we must have a minimum 4,500 feet cloud base. This means that the clouds must not be lower than 4,500 feet, otherwise the spectators won't be able to see all the formations. We have a rolling display for a 2,500 feet cloud base, and a flat display for a cloud base of 1,000 feet. If the clouds are below 1,000 feet we have to call off the display. The three programmes are interchangeable and we can switch from one to another if the weather changes while we're giving a display.

Do you have many accidents?

No, very, very rarely.

What's the most difficult manoeuvre you have to do?

It may surprise you, but it's taking off and landing.

Are the aircraft insured?

No. The aircraft, as items, are not insured. They are worth just under one million pounds each.

How many planes do you have?

In addition to the nine in the team, there are two spares. The Team Manager pilots one of the spare aircraft during transit flights.

Do you have any spare pilots?

No. If one of the team is ill, we do a display with 8 aircraft.

How much fuel can a plane take?

We can carry 350 gallons of aviation fuel which weighs 1,350 kilograms, but we don't often take off with full tanks. We only carry as much as we need for a particular flight plus some in reserve.

What's your top speed?

Mach 1.02 or 633 miles an hour in level flight.

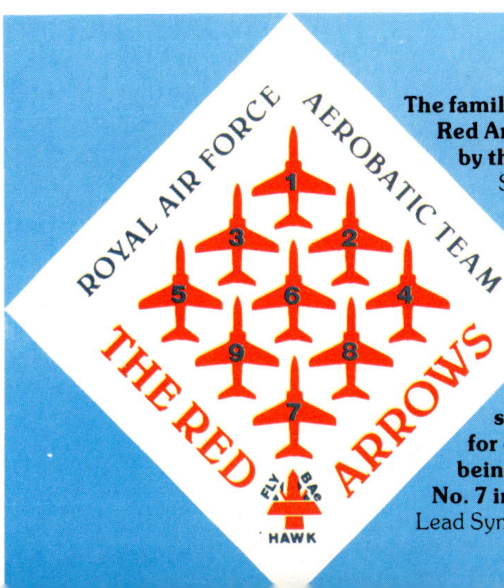

The familiar Diamond formation of the Red Arrows. No. 1 aircraft is piloted by the Leader. **Nos. 6 and 7 are the** Synchro Pair **which break away from the other seven during the display to do the spectacular 'pairs' aerobatics. The three 'new' pilots who join the team in the autumn fly at Nos. 8, 9 and 4 or 5 in their first season. A pilot will have flown for one year with the team before being eligible to fly at** Synchro 2 **at No. 7 in his second year, and then as** Lead Synchro **at No. 6 in his third year.**

Learning about the parts of a wing . . .

How long a runway does a Hawk need?

The aircraft can be stopped in about 3,000 feet, but we normally use 6,000 feet as our standard runway length.

Do you have a rehearsal of the display at each location?

No . . . but let's go to the Navigation Room and I'll show you how we do it.

Looking at the Ram Air Turbine (RAT) which either supplements or runs the aircraft's hydraulic system if its 'normal' system fails.

The boys followed Fl. Lt. Myers into another room, on one wall of which was a large map. He told the Cubs that RAF Kemble had its own airspace within a five mile radius of the station. There were, however, two 'special' areas close by — Princess Anne's home at Gatcombe Park and Prince Charles' house at Highgrove. Next to the map one noticeboard gave details of diversionary airfields, Royal flights, etc. and another displayed the latest weather information. Fl. Lt. Myers unrolled a 1:50000 scale map on the map table.

We often give displays at places we've not visited before, so we need to be fully briefed on every aspect of the display area. We have large scale maps and aerial photographs of the terrain from which we can identify all the features we'll need to look for. We then superimpose a transparent overlay of Kemble over the display area, so we'll know exactly where we should be at every stage of the programme.

The next stop on the boys' 'guided tour' was the Safety Equipment Room. They inspected a lifejacket with such features as a whistle, a light which ran on a sea water activated battery, a two-way radio, a special search and rescue transmitter, mini-flares, a heliograph for flashing messages using the sun, razor blades for cutting parachute shrouds and a first aid kit. There was also an attachment which, when pulled, automatically inflated a life raft stowed under the pilot's seat.

Inspecting the nose wheel . . .

What about tall chimneys and things like that?

Someone always surveys the display area on the ground and makes a detailed report back to us.

Do you ever get to a place early or late?

Our flights are very carefully planned so we should arrive within 10 seconds of the time we've said we'll be there.

How do people book you to appear?

Displays are arranged up to two years ahead. The Ministry of Defence decides what our programme will be.

How much do you charge for appearing?

Depending upon the type of display, the organisers will be asked to pay about £2,000 for the performance. Special displays like the RAF Battle of Britain or the Farnborough International Air Show are funded by the Ministry of Defence.

How long could someone survive in the dinghy?

A lot would depend on the conditions and we would normally expect to be picked up very quickly when operating within the United Kingdom. But we could reasonably expect to exist for two or three days in the dinghy, without too many problems.

Does the dinghy have an oar?

No, but there is a sea anchor which helps to prevent the dinghy from drifting.

The boys then had a good look at a helmet with its two special visors (one clear and one tinted), ear seals, microphone, oxygen supply and anti-G supply . . .

What's anti-G mean?

G stands for gravity. If a plane goes into a sudden steep climb, turn or dive the blood will be forced from the pilot's head and he'd black out. An anti-G suit forces the blood to stay in the upper part of the body by exerting pressure on

The boys spent some time in the control tower . . .

. . . and went onto the balcony when an Air Traffic Controller fired a 'bird scarer' cartridge.

Two of the Crash Section's larger vehicles.

the legs and trunk. We get used to the sensation so on most flights we don't need anti-G suits. When we're flying in cold areas or on long journeys we wear up to four layers as it can be very cold at high altitudes. On these flights, the top layer is completely waterproof: we call it a goon suit! By the way, this red suit I'm wearing is very special. It's made of a fireproof material called *Nomex* which is the same as that used by racing car drivers.

One piece of equipment which really caught the Cubs' imagination was a demonstration ejector seat.

How do you make sure it doesn't go off accidentally?

There's a seat firing safety pin which is only taken out just before take off.

How do you actually make it work?

You pull a handle which is just under the seat between your legs.

What happens then?

The top of the canopy is blasted away by small explosives so there's a hole through which the seat can go. A gun shoots the seat up, and a fraction of a second later rockets fire to take the seat clear of the plane and out of its slip stream. The parachute, pilot and dinghy automatically separate from the seat.

Have you ever ejected?

No, I haven't had to.

How much does an ejector seat cost?

About £18,000.

Can you eject when you're flying upside down?

Yes. You could also eject when you're on the ground. The rockets would take you and the seat up to between 200 and 300 feet in 1½ seconds. Now I think it's time we had something to eat.

After lunch in the crew's dining room, the Cubs went outside to take a closer look at Fl. Lt. Myer's Hawk. They took turns to sit in the pilot's seat and Fl. Lt. Myers told them about the array of instruments in the cockpit. The boys were particularly interested in the smoke buttons.

We can make three colours of smoke – red, white and blue.

How is the smoke actually made?

There's a smoke pod mounted on the underside. In the smoke pod there's diesel fuel and two liquid dyes. When one of the buttons is pressed, air pressure inside the tank forces out a mixture of fuel and the appropriate coloured dye. White smoke is produced by injecting ordinary diesel fuel into the jet efflux at the rear of the jet pipe.

As the photographs show, the boys then went round the aircraft from nose to tail – and underneath!

Are the tyres solid or pumped up?

They're pumped up to a pressure of about 160lbs. per square inch.

What happens if you drop something in the cockpit while you're flying?

You don't lean down and pick it up. You just turn the aircraft upside down and pick it off the roof!

Can you have your flying licence endorsed?

No – just taken away . . . but at least we can't be fined for speeding!

The Cubs were then taken across the airfield by car to the control tower where Air Traffic Controller Fl. Lt. W. R. Marnane showed them round the operations room before they went up some stairs to the glass sided room from

Kingsley tried on Fireman Paul Bushell's special fire helmet.

In the Maintenance Section the boys watched a Hawk's undercarriage being tested . . .

. . . saw an engine being changed . . .

. . . and even looked inside an aircraft's engine bay!

Nicholas presented Fl. Lt. John Myers with a plaque on behalf of all readers of the CUB SCOUT ANNUAL.

which all aircraft coming into or flying out of RAF Kemble are 'controlled'. They looked at the radar scanners, peered through binoculars, and listened to the radio conversations between the tower and pilots. They were also given a demonstration of the Verey light pistol which is used as a means of communication when there is no radio contact. A red flare means 'Go away'; a green flare means 'You are free to land'; a yellow flare means 'We are signalling'. The boys were advised to cover their ears when a bird scarer cartridge was detonated.

Why do you need to scare off birds?

If a bird is sucked into the air intake it can do a lot of damage to the rotating blades of the turbine inside the engine.

A little later the boys would see the effect of a bird strike, but their next port of call was the Crash Section. Station Fire Officer Dolby and Fireman Paul Bushell showed them the various vehicles which have to be able to reach any part of the airfield in two minutes to deal with an emergency.

The Cubs were driven back to the huge hangars and the Maintenance Section where Fl. Lt. Myers rejoined them. The engine of one of the Hawks was being changed because a bird had been sucked in during a flight that morning. The boys certainly got a bird's eye view of an engine and the engine bay!

How much does one of these engines cost?

About £250,000.

What sort of engine is it?

It's a specially modified Rolls Royce 'Adour' Mark 151 engine with a twin-spool turbo-fan.

How long does it take to change an engine?

Between six and eight hours.

How many spare engines do you have?

Two, so we have a total of 13 engines.

The Cubs examined a smoke pod, taking great care not to get dye on their clothes.

'It's almost impossible to get out,' Fl. Lt. Myers warned them.

Their very eventful day was almost over. The boys returned to the Crew Room where they were photographed with all the Red Arrows pilots. Nicholas then presented Fl. Lt. Myers with a plaque, the inscription on which read:

THANK YOU
FROM THE CUB
SCOUTS WHO VISITED
THE RED ARROWS IN
1982 FOR A FEATURE
IN THE 1984 CUB
SCOUT ANNUAL

Each Cub was given posters, stickers, and a photograph signed by the team. Their day with the Red Arrows had come to an end.

THE CUB SCOUT ANNUAL gratefully acknowledges the help and co-operation of RAF Kemble, and all the Red Arrows team (particularly Flight Lieutenant John Myers) without whose assistance this feature would not have been possible.

Special note: During 1983 the Red Arrows home base was moved from RAF Kemble in Gloucestershire to RAF Scampton in Lincolnshire.

The Hawks parked outside their hanger at RAF Kemble – this is a view from underneath the Hercules aircraft which usually accompanied the team. However, when we were there in the summer of '82, the Hercules was on service in the South Atlantic.

Historic Mail Coach Run

This year (1984) the Post Office will be bringing back the mail coach – but just for a day!

The Post Office will be re-enacting the first Royal Mail coach run between Bristol and London in August, to celebrate the bi-centenary of its introduction.

The coach to be used in the run was built in the early 19th century and has been restored by John Parker of Diss, Norfolk, who will drive the coach, with its four horses, on the historic journey.

In all, 20 horses will be needed to make the run between Bristol and London and 24 grooms to attend them.

So much work was needed to re-enact the mail coach journey that the Post Office started planning two years ago.

As the run will be done to the original times the teams of horses must be changed in less than two minutes at the stopping points to keep to the timetable. The horses have been trained to do the night part of the run and be used to cameras and lighting as the Post Office expects the full glare of publicity!

Some of the old mail coach roads no longer exist and at certain places the existing roads, as near the route as possible, will be used.

HOW IT ALL STARTED

The Post Office really began for this country when people besides the King wanted to send messages. The growth of trade in medieval Europe made this come about.

Merchants used their own private messengers and sometimes got the King's messenger to carry letters for them. Besides these merchants and noblemen there were few people in the country who could even write their own names!

In 1591 Queen Elizabeth I announced that all letters going overseas could only be carried by the Royal messengers. This was because merchants might be Spanish Catholics or Dutch Protestants and often acted as agents for foreign countries. This country's Government, therefore, wanted to know what letters being sent abroad said!

By 1609 Queen Elizabeth's successor, James I, had extended this law to internal letters as well and carrying letters had become a State monopoly.

The service was, however, painfully slow – it could take about 17 hours to ride from Winchester to Southampton.

By the 1780s trade and industry wanted replies to letters within 48 hours rather than three or four days.

In 1782 John Palmer, a theatre manager from Bath, noted that coaches did the London to Bristol run in 17 hours. The post, by postboy, still took two days.

In 1784 John Palmer approached the Government with a scheme for using special lightweight coaches to replace the postboys and in that year his scheme was adopted.

Agreement was signed in July 1784 in connection with Palmer's scheme, under which five inn keepers – one each in London, Thatcham and Marlborough and two in Bath – agreed to provide the horses. The first mail coach run took place in August 1784, starting from the Swan with Two Necks inn at London at 8.00 pm, arriving at the Three Tuns inn at Bath before 10.00 am the next morning and reaching the Rummer Tavern, Bristol, by 12.00 midday.

For the return journey the mail left Bristol from the Swan Tavern at 4.00 pm to arrive in London before 8.00 am next morning.

The first journey from London to Bristol took 16 hours, breaking previous passenger coach records.

With the mail coach the postal service entered a new age. Palmer's service on the London – Bath – Bristol route quickly spread throughout the country. Palmer was appointed by the Post Office to run the new services.

The actual coaches were hired from contractors – only the guard was a Post Office worker. He was equipped with the famous Post Horn which warned tollgate keepers to open their gates (tolls were free for mail coaches) and to tell postmasters that the coach was entering town.

Mail coaches continued in use until the next great force for change – the railway.

The Bristol Royal Mail in King Street, Bristol in about 1830. Built in Temple Street, Bristol, this coach carried the Royal Mail between Bristol, Bath and London.

The Age of Steam

written and illustrated by Peter Stuckey

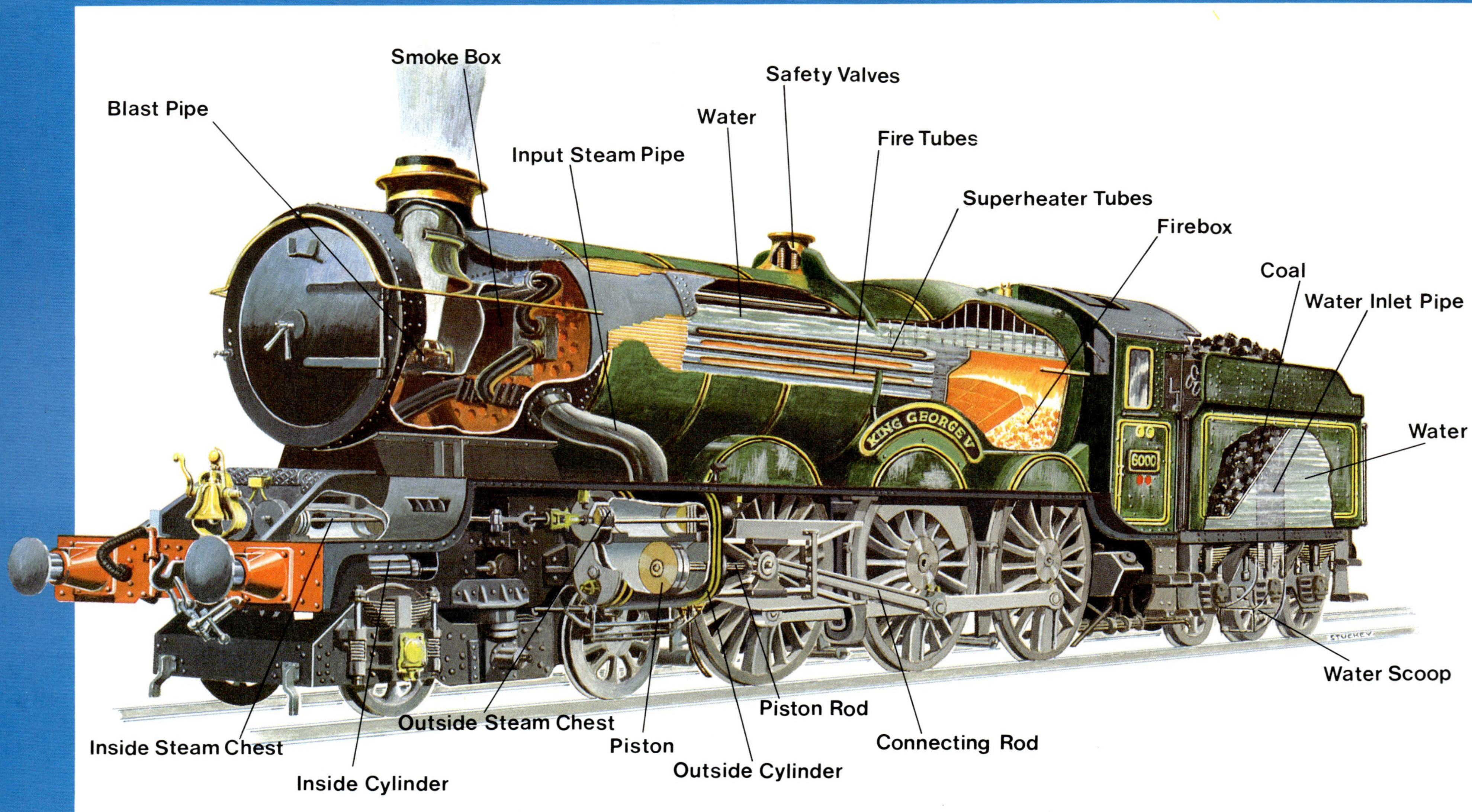

The Age of Steam really began in 1698 when Thomas Savery built the first steam driven pump. However the use of steam power did not become practicable until 1712 when Thomas Newcomen applied it to his first beam engine. He harnessed steam to operate a rocking beam which in turn worked a pump. The pump drained water from the Cornish tin mines which were always in danger of flooding.

Newcomen's invention was soon taken up and improved upon by a Scottish instrument maker called James Watt. He eventually found a way to make the rocking beam turn a large wheel, thus providing the means to drive machinery in mills and factories. So began the Industrial Revolution in the 18th Century. It was not long before steam was being employed in all sorts of ways to replace water, horse and man-power. It is interesting that James Watt adopted the term 'horse power' for the unit of measuring the power of a steam engine.

In 1804 a mining engineer named Richard Trevithick built the first steam locomotive to run on rails and it was used for pulling a 'train' of mine wagons. The steam railway had arrived. Three years later an American, Robert Fulton, put a steam engine in a boat to drive a pair of paddle-wheels. This was a success and foretold the inevitable end of the sailing ship.

From that time onwards the design of steam engines improved rapidly and the use of steam power has now become a highly developed technology which today is used to drive great turbines in huge ships, submarines and power stations which generate electricity – far removed from the simple engines of Newcomen and Watt but still using exactly the same basic principles.

To many people the Age of Steam means the great steam locomotives which once operated our railways. One of the most famous classes of engine in Great Britain was the 4 cylinder, 6000, 4-6-0 'King' class. '4-6-0' is the way of describing the wheel arrangement, meaning that the locomotive is fitted with two pairs of free-running 'bogie' wheels and three pairs of driving wheels with no 'bogie' wheels at the rear end.

Our cut-away drawing shows the well known locomotive 'KING GEORGE V', which is now preserved in working condition. It was built in 1927 and worked until 1962 with nearly two million miles to its credit. In 1927 it visited the United States of America for the one hundredth anniversary celebrations of the Baltimore and Ohio Railroad, when it was presented with its famous bell – a feature of all American locomotives – and a momento it proudly carries on its buffer beam to this day.

How a Steam Engine works

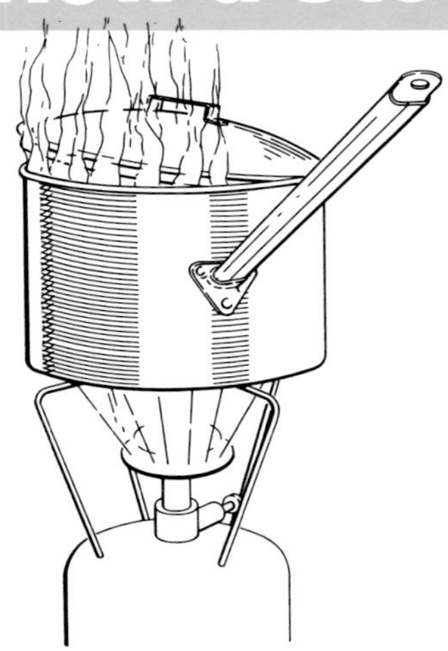

The steam produced from water boiling in a saucepan can lift the saucepan lid. This is the basis of the steam engine. The steam engine is really just a big kettle with a built-in fire, to produce steam which is directed through pipes, valves and cylinders to push on pistons – or turbine blades – which in turn work machines.

This is a very simple diagram showing how steam can be translated into work.

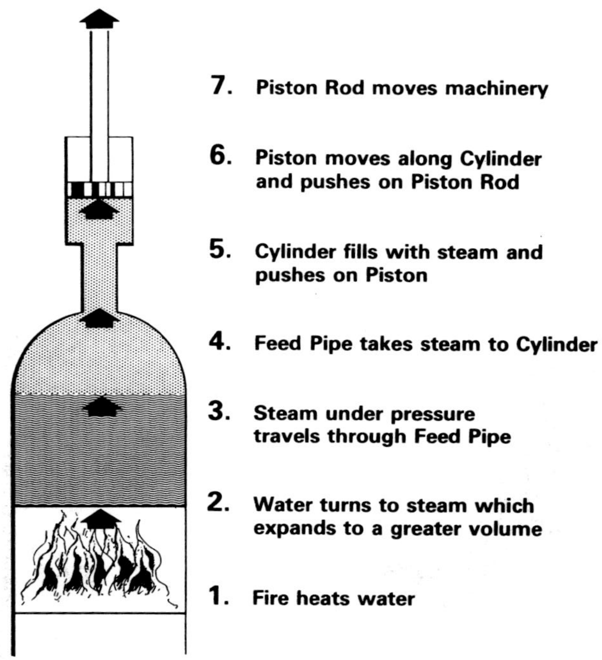

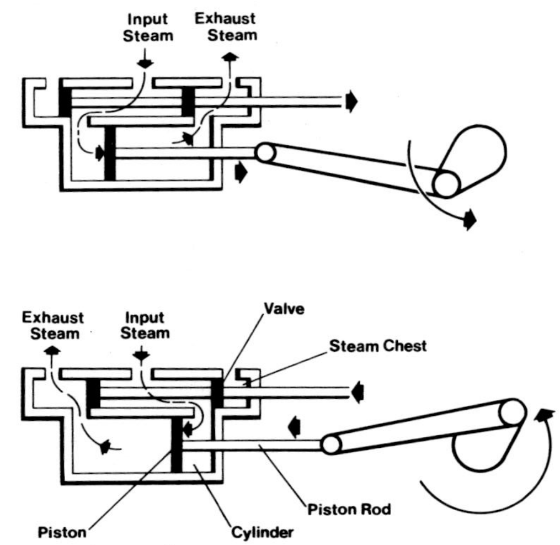

Diagrams showing two stages in the working cycle of a steam locomotive, using one type of 'double-acting' cylinder and valve arrangement. There are other arrangements but they all do basically the same job.
A 'double-acting' cylinder is one in which the steam can be made to push on the piston from either side as the valve moves backwards and forwards, uncovering each inlet and exhaust 'port' in turn on either side of the piston. The steam locomotive shown in our coloured picture uses four such cylinders.

Nine Men's Morris

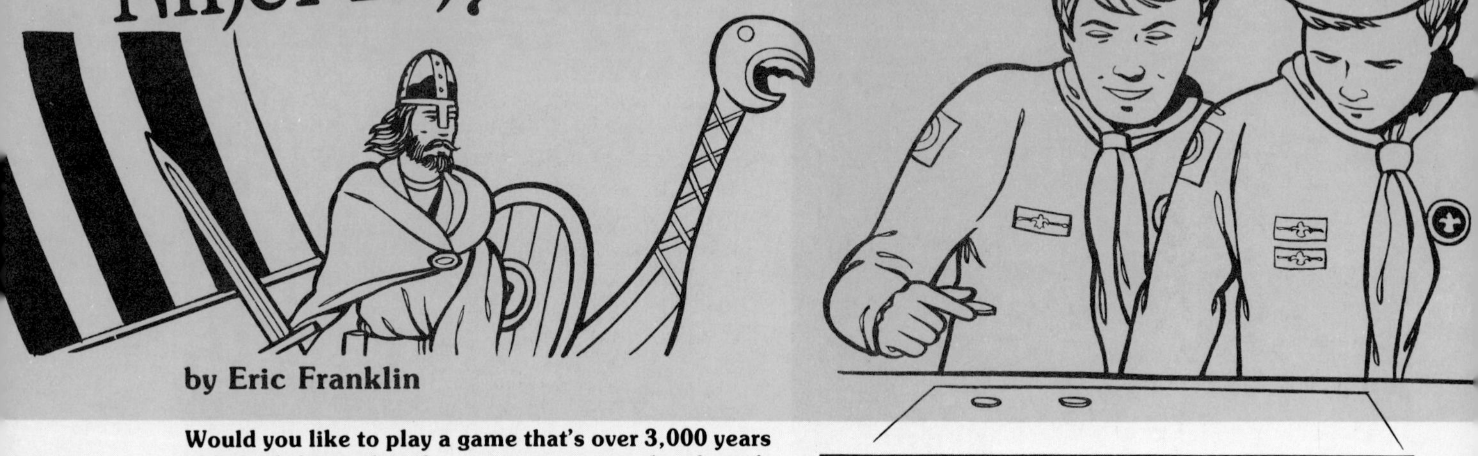

by Eric Franklin

Would you like to play a game that's over 3,000 years old, that's been played in many countries, that doesn't need elaborate apparatus, and that has fairly simple rules? Such a game is Nine Men's Morris.

Reference to this game was made in some carvings dating back to 1400 B.C. and in Sri Lanka (formerly Ceylon) the design was cut into some steps which were laid down about 20 A.D. where it was used as a charm against evil. It has been found on old Roman tiles, on an ancient tombstone in the Isle of Man and at many other places in various countries. Shakespeare mentions it in his play *A Midsummer Night's Dream:* 'The nine men's morris is filled up with mud'. It has even been carved in the choir stalls of an English cathedral . . . did the choir boys years ago play during the sermon, I wonder?

Making the game

To play the game you will need a board and 18 counters – nine of one colour for one player, and nine of another colour for the other player. The counters could be black and white draughtsmen, bottletops painted with enamel in different colours, buttons, etc.
To make the board you will need a sheet of fairly stiff cardboard *or* plywood *or* laminated plastic 24cm square.

Then follow these instructions:

1. With a pencil lightly draw parallel lines 3cm apart.

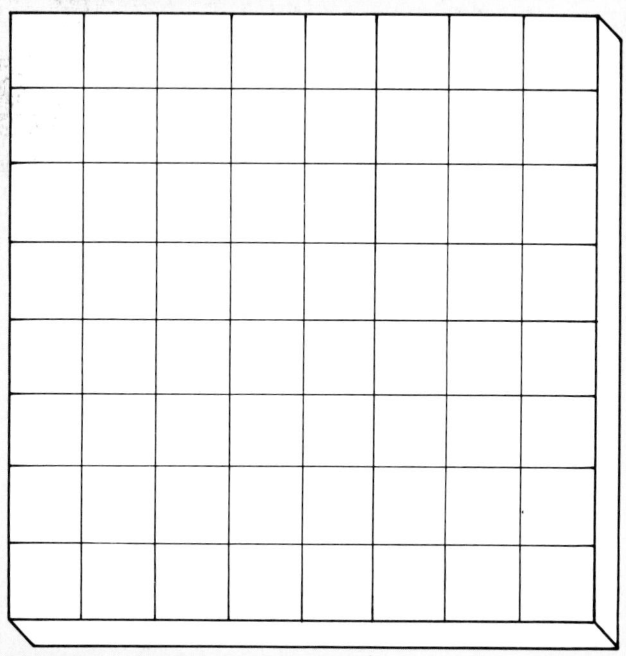

2. Turn the board through 90° and draw similar lines.

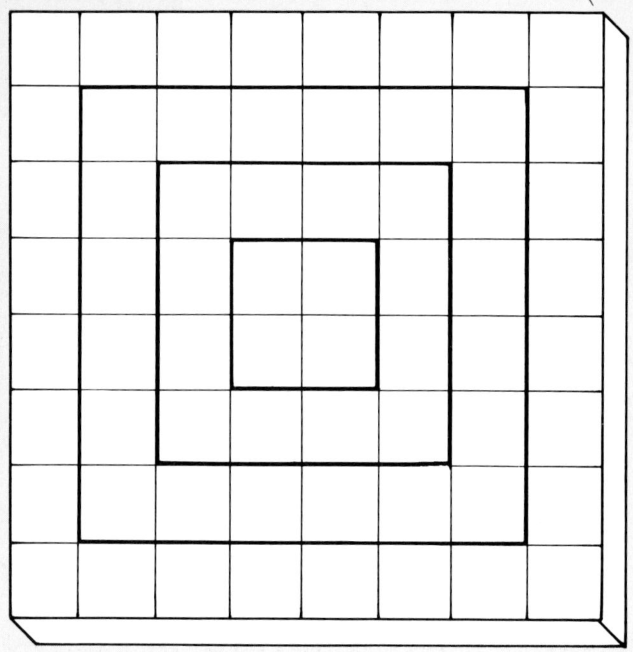

3. With a pen and permanent ink or ballpoint pen go over the lines shown in this diagram.

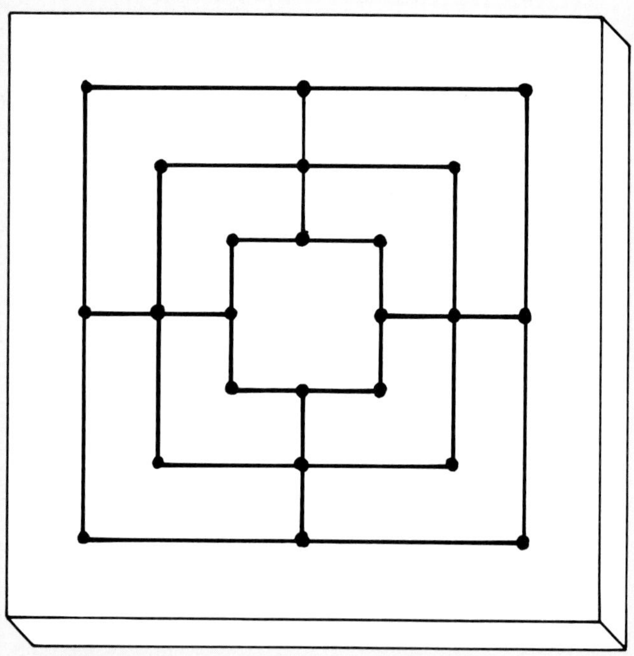

4. Mark the exact centre of each of the inked lines, and draw in the remaining four lines. Carefully rub out the pencil lines to leave the finished board.

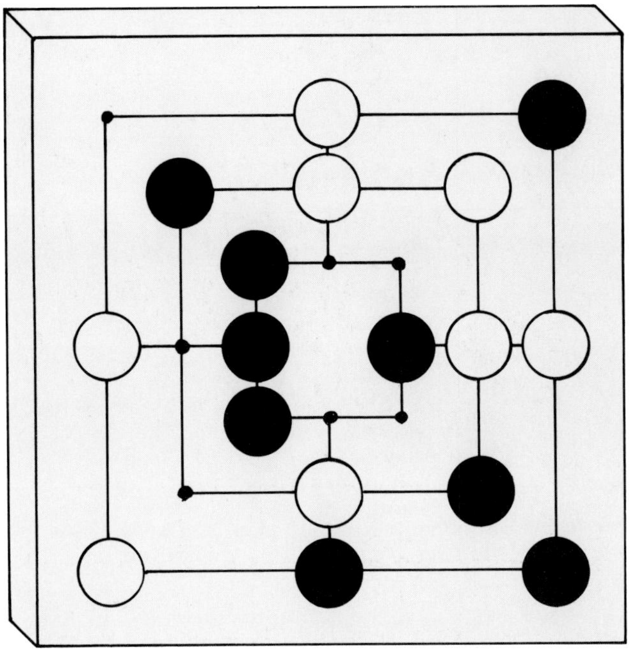

If you are making the board from wood or plastic, it is a good idea to score the lines first with a scriber or sharp point and then to ink them in. (Ask your parents for help.) The board can be cleaned with fine sandpaper without rubbing out any inked lines.

How to play the game

The game is for two players. On the board there are 24 bases. Horizontally, vertically and diagonally there are 16 lines, with three bases each. The players start by alternately placing their nine counters, one at a time, on vacant bases, with the object of trying to get three-in-a-row. This is achieved by placing three consecutive counters on any line of bases.

As soon as a player gets three-in-a-row he can 'impound' one of his opponent's counters – that is, he can take any one of his opponent's counters off the board – *except* a counter that forms part of an opponent's three-in-a-row.

When all 18 counters have been placed the players move their counters about – one counter at a time, in turn – trying to get three-in-a-row. These moves can only be made on the lines, one space at a time.

When a player has only three counters left on the board, he has the privilege of hopping to *any* vacant base he may choose. For example, he can jump across the board with the object of blocking his opponent – and then, with his next turn, move back to his three-in-a-row.

A player wins the game when his opponent has only two counters left.

Post script

You can also play Nine Men's Morris out-of-doors on a design scratched in sand or earth. Stones, shells or pebbles can be used for counters.

How to play the Safety Game

(see back cover)

On the back cover of your Annual there's a board on which you can play The Safety Game. It's not only a great game which can be played with any number of players, but it's also a game from which you might learn something!

What you will need

A small coloured disc or object for each player
A spinner with six sides or a dice

How to play

1. Decide the order in which the players are going to play.
2. Throw the dice or spin the spinner and move your disc or counter the number of squares shown on the dice or spinner.
3. Follow the instructions (if any) written in the square on which you land.
4. The winner is the first person to reach the FINISH. A player *must* get the exact number to reach square 40. For example, if you are on square 35 you cannot move to the finish by throwing a '6'; you would need a '5' to finish in one move: from square 38 you will need a '2' to complete the game.

> **Special Note**
>
> There are a few really nasty squares! For example, if you land on 37 you will have to go back to 28 . . . back to 20 . . . back to 12 in one move! We have done this quite deliberately to make the game more interesting.

By the way . . .

We've said that we hope you might learn something from this game. Look at the instructions in the squares and work out *why* either you have to pay a penalty and go back, or you are allowed to move forward. We've only been able to include a few safety points from around the home, and near or in the road and water. What other safety factors do you know?

Always remember that it's not a matter of what you know, but what you do. Never forget that in real life nowhere and nothing is ever completely safe – be on your guard!

IT'S A CUB'S LIFE!

Illustrated by Leslie Cecil

Dem bones

Since I joined the Cubs in September we have played rounders, planted a bulb, learned the Grand Howl and put on a sketch. We were skeletons in black with luminous bones. We sang 'Dem bones, dem bones, dem dry bones' and did the actions all in the

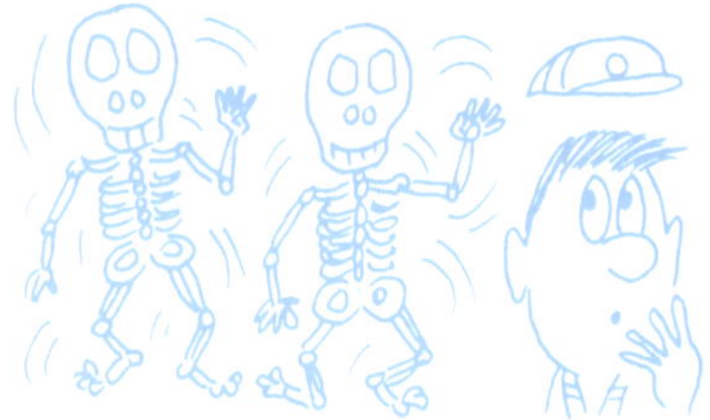

dark. We also sang carols and gave presents to older church members.
MARK HINDESS,
3rd Rhiwbina (All Saints), Cardiff.

Robbed

On my first camping trip something terrible happened. The first night the shop was robbed. Two groups of our Pack saw him.
CHRIS CORNISH,
7th Rotherham, Yorkshire.

Spectacular

My favourite Cub event was our visit to York Minster where I had the opportunity to ring the fourth largest bell in the world and rang 'Great Peter' (the noise was almost deafening) in St. Peter's Tower. It was a tremendous thrill to climb to the top of the Minster and see the spectacular sight of York which, at the time, was surrounded by floods – a sight I will always remember.
ANDREW JOHNSON,
3rd Haxby and Wiggington, York.

Water-fall

The best time was when we had to climb up a waterfall and we all slipped. It was fun.
NIGEL HEALEY,
Heywood, Lancashire.

Exciting

Three packs from Tavistock went to London to see the Royal Tournament. It was very good with all the white helmets, stunts, the guns and the bands. After the show we went to Baden-Powell House where we looked at some old badges and had our tea. Later we bought souvenirs before leaving for a sightseeing tour around London. Finally it was time to go home after a very exciting day.
BRENDAN CLEMENS,
1st Tavistock (Kestrels), Devon.

Entertainment

At Christmas our Pack entertained the old people at Puttenhoe. We did a lot of practice beforehand when we were divided into four groups. At the beginning we sang some camp fire songs together accompanied by the rhythm group. The shadowgraph group did the Nativity story. Next the poetry group said some poems. During the interval we talked to the old people. This was followed by the musicians' group when I played my clarinet. At the end our Commissioner

presented each of us with our Entertainer Proficiency Badge. The old people said that they had enjoyed it very much.
HOWARD JACOBS,
1st Puttenhoe (Panthers), Bedford.

Bombers

Before Christmas we went trampolining. Last Friday we played Bombers Overhead. If the Cub Leader says "Bombers Overhead" you lie on your tummy and put your hands on your head. If he says "Submarines" you lie on your back with one leg up in the air. If he says "Women and children" you pick someone up. If he says "Aye! Aye! Captain!" you say that. The last person to do the thing is out.
ALASDAIR GILLIES,
43rd Edinburgh.

The ugliest mug

Last year on St. George's Day I went with my Pack to the District Parade and Service at a local church. It's an old church with gargoyles around it. The vicar talked about them and then asked us all to pull ugly faces like the gargoyles. He liked mine best and he took me to the front of the church for

everyone to see. Later on a photographer from the local paper called at our house and took two photographs of me – one pulling an ugly face, and one of me normally. I was a celebrity next Pack Meeting because I made the front page.
MICHAEL BURGESS,
36th Salford (Claremont),
Lancashire.

Aussie muck about

My Cub Pack and some other Packs went on a Cub Muck-About. There was boating, a giant flying fox and a commando course. We also cooked dampers and sausages in bread. It was a very exciting day and we all enjoyed it very much.
DALE LEBOEUF,
3rd Dingley, Victoria, Australia.

Did you see the first page of It's a Cub's Life on page 8?

VISITORS FROM SPACE

by Tilly Wingrave

Illustrated by Martin Aitchison

Akela was laughing when he came out of the stores tent. "You know," he said to Baloo, "I believe they eat more every time we bring them to camp!"

He walked to his tent, collected his anorak, and then went across to the Cubs who were playing rounders.

"Baloo and I are going to the village for some more food," he said, fastening the zip of his anorak, "otherwise there won't be any dinner tomorrow! Rikki's in his tent sorting out some things for the camp fire. So you behave yourselves. We shan't be long."

Akela and Baloo made their way to the Group's mini-bus which was parked in the shade of a tree. The Cubs waved as the two Leaders drove down the stony track and disappeared round a bend which led onto the main road.

★ ★ ★

Two miles above the surface of the Earth, the spaceship hovered silently on its anti-gravity motors. Captain Kron received reports from his crew.

"This is the third planet in this solar system, and the only one capable of supporting Dril life," reported First Officer Grat.

"The planet is inhabited," said Second Officer Frip. "There is a small settlement just below us. It appears to be quite primitive, and should present no difficulties."

Kron drew himself up to his full four feet six inches. He was tall for a Dril. "At last!" he exclaimed. "I have found a new colony for Drila! The planet will be named Kron, of course," he added smugly.

The ship began its silent descent towards the green surface of the planet.

The game of rounders had ended. The Cubs lay stretched out on the grass, eyes closed against the bright sunshine.

"What shall we do now?" asked Ian.

Opening his eyes, Colin sat up and looked round at the camp site. To the north and east the meadow was bounded by a wood, while to the south the ground sloped steeply down towards a stream at the bottom of the valley. A barbed wire fence divided the western side from the track which led to the main road.

"You know," he said, "this would make a smashing fort! Tell you what! My side will be the Cavalry defending the fort, and your side can be the Indians attacking us. Like that film we saw on television last week!"

The idea was greeted with enthusiasm. Ian collected his 'Indians' and began to move away.

"Give us time to get ready before you attack," Colin called.

"It's all right," answered Ian. "We're going down to the stream first. There are some reeds there that we can use to make Indian head-dresses."

As Ian and his party disappeared, Colin and the others began to build barricades from kit bags, rolled up sleeping bags, and any other likely looking objects. Rikki poked his head out of the tent, saw what the boys were doing and, having satisfied himself that they were keeping out of mischief, retreated into his tent to get on with the camp fire programme.

"Here they come!" shouted young Steven, who had been posted as look-out.

"They haven't given us much time," grumbled Colin. He glanced at the figures approaching along the track. "Wait a minute!" he exclaimed. "That's not them. It's some other boys. They must be from the village."

The visitors hesitated at the gate, then came into the camp. The tallest of them stepped forward. "Greetings," he said, making a strange circular movement with his hands. "We come in peace."

"Oh, er . . . hello," answered Colin uncertainly. "Nice to see you."

"May we look round your settlement?" asked the visitor politely.

"Yes, if you like," said Colin.

"They're all dressed the same," whispered Steven, as the Cubs watched the strangers inspecting the camp. "I wonder where they got those funny shiny anoraks."

For some reason they didn't go over to the Scouters' tents, and when they had completed their tour the visitors went into a huddle at the far side of the camp.

"It must always be very hot here," said Frip. "The dwellings are made from a woven fabric."

"The cooking arrangements are very primitive," reported Grat, "yet the metal cooking utensils suggest quite a high degree of technology. A very strange mixture!"

"I have noticed something even more strange," said Kron. "They have no weapons!"

"What! Not even for hunting? But that is impossible!" gasped Grat.

Ian and his Indians chose that moment to attack. With wild whoops they burst out of the woods, brandishing bows and arrows made from reeds. They had more reeds stuck in their headbands and their faces were streaked with lines of mud from the stream. Ian had insisted that his tribe should wear 'war paint' so that they'd look like *real* Indians.

"Now we shall see if they have weapons!" observed Kron.

The first casualty of the battle was Steven, struck by a reed arrow. He fell to the ground with a blood-curdling scream and 'died' in a way that would have won an award for any TV actor.

"The vegetation must be highly poisonous!" exclaimed Frip. "We must take care to avoid it."

By now the 'cavalry' had got themselves organised. Completely forgetting the visitors, they flung themselves behind their barricades, made finger guns, and began firing at the Indians.

"Pah! Pah!" shouted Colin, pointing at two Indians in turn. The two fell to the ground, writhing in agony, and clutching their 'wounds'.

The others were equally good shots, and soon the ground was strewn with rapidly expiring Indians.

"No wonder they have no weapons," gasped Kron. "They have only to point a finger and their victim dies in agony!"

The battle was quickly over, Big Chief Ian and his remaining braves being taken prisoner.

"Well, at least we took you by surprise," remarked Ian.

"Only because we were talking to those other boys," retorted Colin.

"What boys?"

"Those boys over there," Colin replied, pointing his index finger towards the horrified Drils.

"Quick!" exclaimed Grat. "They are attacking us!"

With cries of terror, the Drils turned and ran for the woods. The boys could hear them crashing panic-stricken through the undergrowth.

"What made them do that?" asked Colin in bewilderment.

"I'm glad they've gone," said Steven. "They were a funny lot!"

"Let's play the game again," suggested Ian, "only this time you lot can be the Indians."

Before Colin could answer, Steven shouted: "Look!"

From somewhere behind the wood, a huge silver shape rose silently into the air. Slowly at first, but quickly gathering speed, it rose higher and higher into the sky, until it disappeared from sight.

"A Flying Saucer!" breathed Steven.

"If we hadn't been talking to those boys we might have seen it before, and perhaps got a closer look at it," Colin grumbled in disgust. "Now we shall never know what the men in Flying Saucers look like!"

CLIFF BROWN'S PUZZLE PAGE

YOU WILL FIND MORE OF CLIFF BROWN'S PUZZLES ON PAGES 6–42–57.

ANSWERS ON PAGE 63.

WHAT IS IT?

HIDDEN IN THIS MOSAIC IS THE SILHOUETTE OF A MAGNIFICENT BEAST! BLACK IN THOSE SHAPES IN WHICH THERE IS A DOT AND FIND OUT WHAT IT IS.

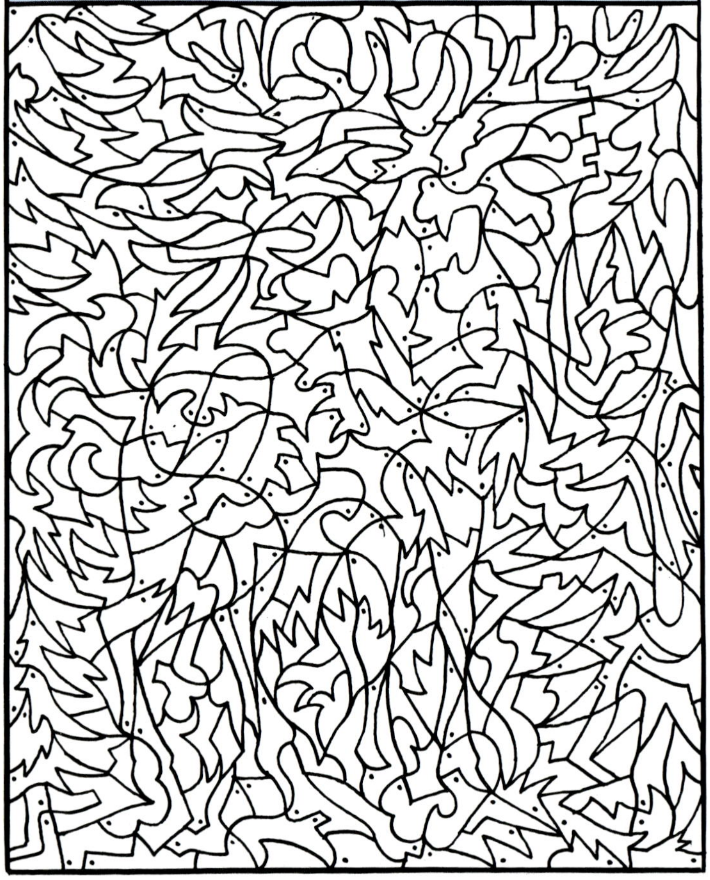

'ERE'S AN 'OWLER!

THIS IS A PICTURE OF A LONG EARED OWL WHICH HAS BEEN CUT INTO STRIPS AND SOMEHOW BECOME ALL MIXED UP. **WITHOUT** CUTTING UP THE PICTURE CAN YOU WORK OUT THE CORRECT ORDER AND SAY WHICH STRIPS ARE UPSIDE DOWN?

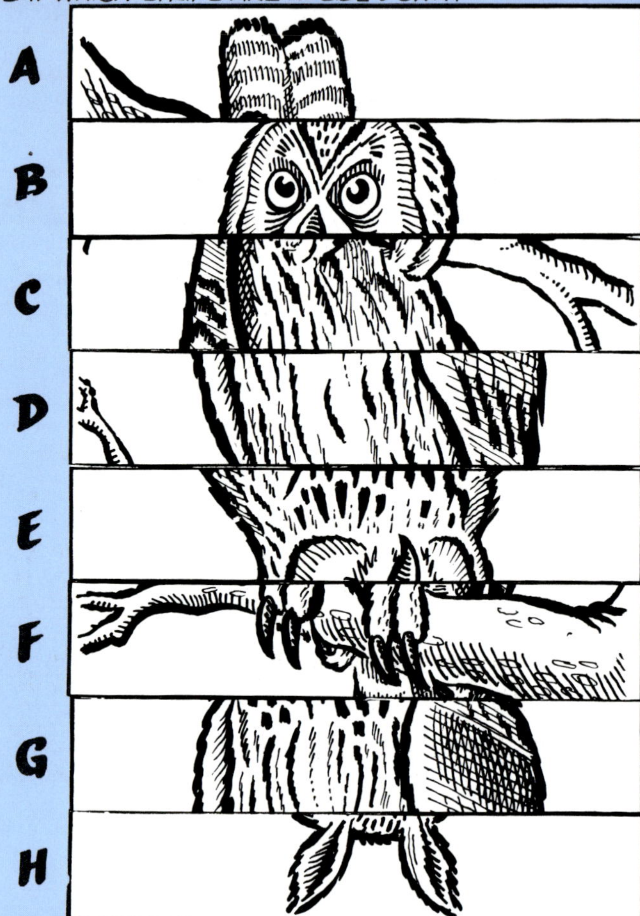

MIXED-UP BRITISH WILDLIFE

IN THE PICTURE BELOW YOU CAN SEE SEVEN VERY STRANGE CREATURES. EACH ONE IS, IN FACT, A MIXTURE OF TWO BRITISH WILDLIFE SPECIES. CAN YOU NAME ALL FOURTEEN?

When you are a Scout . . .

by Ron Jeffries

If you asked all your friends who are Cub Scouts to tell you the activities they most enjoy in their Packs, you would finish up with a very long list indeed!

I would guess that most will say that they like the games at Pack Meetings. Camps and expeditions will be favourites, too, but after that – well! For some it's map reading or swimming, while others will go for football, modelling, tracking . . . the list will be endless! We are all different!

When you have been in the Pack for a couple of years or so, Akela will talk with you about moving into the Scout Troop. Just as you enjoyed taking part in some activities more than others in the Pack, so it will be in the Troop, but there is a difference.

In the Scout Troop you will be a Member of a Patrol, working as a team at Troop Night, in camp and on expeditions. If you are good at knots or first aid or map reading, your Patrol Leader will want you to use those skills for the benefit of everyone else in the Patrol.

Most of us enjoy doing the things we are good at. In the Pack you've tried your hand at many things, but in your Patrol you will have the chance to learn more about the things you enjoy doing and to become better at those particular skills. For example, if you are good at map reading, your Patrol Leader will want you to work with an older Member of the Patrol in planning and leading a hike. If you like cooking, there will be plenty to keep you busy when you are in camp.

The Link Badge

One of the first things you will do when you are getting ready to move into the Troop is meet your Patrol Leader.

Some of your friends will be in the Troop already – you knew them when they were in the Pack and they will tell you about life in the Scout Troop. Your Patrol Leader will want you to tell him all about yourself and he will want to know what you've learned in the Pack, particularly the things you are good at doing.

You will take the Link Badge while you are still in the Cubs, but it will give you the opportunity to get to know your Patrol Leader and the rest of the Scouts in your new Patrol. Your Patrol Leader will explain the things you need to know – something about how Scouting started, the Scout Promise and Law (and what they mean) and the thing you will most look forward to – an activity with the Patrol.

The activity could be on a local camp site – lighting a fire and cooking your supper. You might go on a short hike with the Patrol or visit a nearby town to explore together.

Troop Night

On Troop Night your Patrol joins with the other Patrols in the Troop for games, for training and a host of activities that you'll enjoy. Sometimes you will be making plans for a Patrol activity during the week or at the weekend.

If the Patrol is going to camp, your Patrol Leader might ask you to work with another Scout in preparing the menu and buying the food, or if it's first aid that you are good at, he may want you to check the Patrol's first aid box and buy any supplies that are needed.

Every Member of the Patrol will have a job to do and when you get to camp it's up to everyone to help out with cooking, collecting wood and all the other things that have to be done.

Adventure plus!

If you enjoyed doing lots of things in the Pack, there's an even wider choice in the Scouts! The sort of activities you and your Patrol try will be up to you to decide. Some will be in the Patrol and others with the rest of the Troop. Turn over the page and we'll show you what we mean . . .

Illustrated by John Paice

Adventure plus!

On these pages are just a few of the many activities to enjoy with your Patrol in the Scout Troop. The Scout Progress Scheme is filled with things to do with your Patrol or with Scouts of your own age – and there are proficiency badges if you want to take a skill further. It's adventure all the way in the Scouts – as you'll soon find out.

Camping: there's a lot to practise before you go to camp – packing your rucsac, pitching a tent, lighting a fire, cooking a meal, lighting stoves, planning menus. When you've been camping a few times, try making a bivouac to sleep the night in and cook your food backwoods-style.

International: with some 16 million Scouts in the world, you've plenty to choose from if you are looking for a pen pal, finding out about his home and country, and perhaps even visiting him one day. Taking part in an International camp in this country or going abroad for the Troop's summer camp are all opportunities not to be missed.

Emergencies: knowing how to cope with an emergency is an important part of a Scout's training. Make up your own first aid kit and learn how to deal with accidents you might meet in the home, in the street, at school or in camp. By learning to swim now you could save someone's life later . . .

Hikes and expeditions: using a map and compass and knowing how to read the weather signs are the things to learn at Patrol Meetings. Hiking gives you the chance to meet people and to visit places you've not been to before. Later you can go on expeditions – hiking, cycling or travelling by canoe or boat.

Adventurous activities: sailing, canoeing, hill walking, climbing, ski-ing, caving – these are just a few of the activities that older Scouts enjoy. First, there are many things to learn about equipment, safety precautions and the right way to set about each sport or activity. What you do in your Troop will depend on where you live and if there are expert instructors available. Older Scouts often join with Members of their Venture Scout Units to take part in these activities.

Pioneering: you'll learn your knots and lashings in activities – building fun projects with your Patrol at weekends and in camp. Towers, bridges, rafts – they all give you the chance to try out your skills – and there are rescue knots to learn, too, for when you take part in more adventurous activities as an older Scout or Venture Scout.

Service: the Scout Promise and Law is at the heart of all we do in the Troop – and being concerned for the place where we live and the people in our community is an important part of this. Short-term service projects should be in every Patrol's programme – helping the sick and needy, the handicapped and those who are less fortunate. Taking positive action to clear up eyesores locally helps to improve the environment in which we live.

Hobbies: whatever your hobby, you'll have the opportunity to learn more about it and to share your knowledge with other Scouts in the Troop. There are proficiency badges for many hobbies, too. Often you'll be able to use your hobby to help the Patrol – making equipment if you're keen on carpentry, taking part in the District Sports if you're athletic, keeping the Patrol log book if you enjoy writing and photography . . .

Life in the Troop will be what you make it! Your Scout Leader and the Patrol Leaders will want to make the programme an action-packed time for everyone, so back them up by joining in all the activities that they arrange – and enjoy the Troop!

THE SPACE AGE

devised and drawn by Peter Stuckey

Thirty or forty years ago, few people would have believed that Man would actually walk on the moon or send a rocket beyond the farthest planet. In the last twenty years enormous advances have been made. In this feature you can see just a few of the milestones in Man's exploration of space.

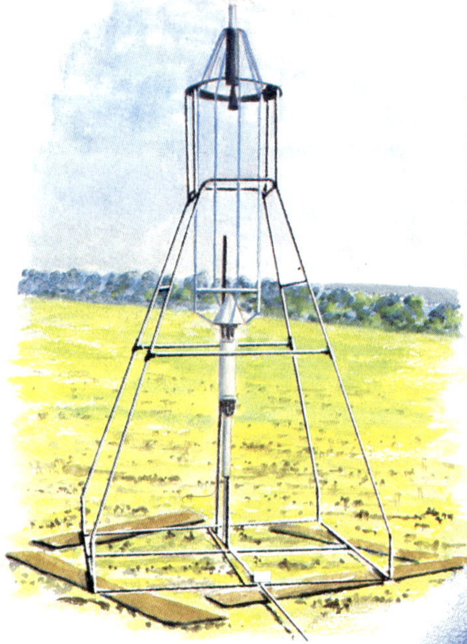

Robert Goddard produced the first liquid fuelled rocket in 1926.

A fictitious moon rocket as described in the science fiction of 1936. Note the 'ski-jump' launching ramp which is nothing like the high vertical towers used to launch the *real* space rockets.

The German V2 rocket was designed by Wernher von Braun and was used as a long range missile in the Second World War.

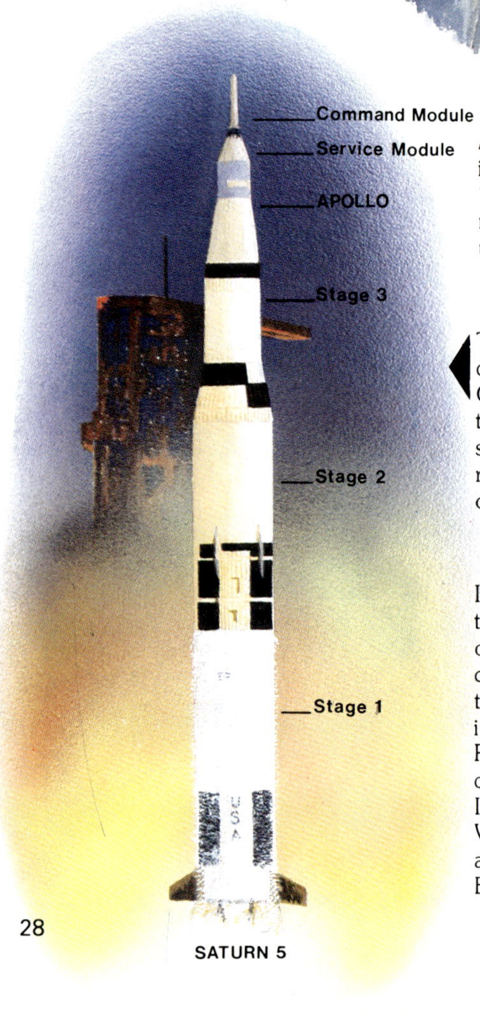

The Saturn 5 rocket of 1968 was a direct descendant of Robert Goddard's rocket *(see above)*. This is typical of the rockets used to launch satellites and space capsules. The rocket discards stages as it moves into outer space.

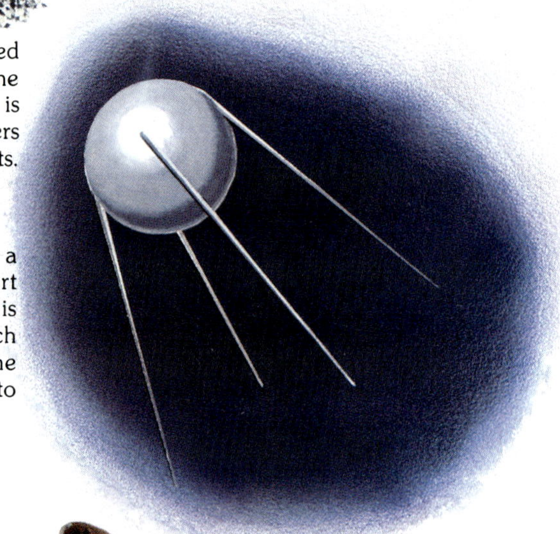

The first artificial satellite to orbit the earth was the Russian Sputnik 1 which was sent up in 1957. Since that time both the Americans and the Russians have put many artificial satellites into orbit as aids to navigation, weather forecasting and communications.

In 1957, the Russians put the first animal into space onboard Sputnik 2. This dog, called Laika, pioneered the way for putting a man into space. In 1961, the Russian Major Yuri Gagarin circled the Earth in Vostok 1. In 1963 a Russian woman, Valentina Tereshkova, achieved 48 orbits of the Earth in Vostok 6.

In 1962 the Americans launched Telstar 1 to transmit television signals to a limited area of the United States of America. By the end of the 1970s a global communications satellite system served nearly 100 countries to exchange television news, telephone calls and business data.

Major Edward White of the United States 'walked' in space from the capsule Gemini 4 in 1965. He remained attached to the the capsule by a gold-plated lifeline.

The first men on the moon were Neil Armstrong and Edwin Aldrin. They descended to the lunar surface from Apollo 2 in the lunar module code named Eagle. A third astronaut, Michael Collins, remained in control of the Command Module. All three returned safely to Earth.

The American Viking Lander sent back pictures from Mars in 1976.

The space shuttle introduced a new era in space exploration. It is a re-usable vehicle designed to travel between Earth and established space stations as a service and transport vehicle. Columbia carried out her first successful space flight in 1981, and her second in 1982.

The launch of a space shuttle with its huge fuel tank and auxilliary rockets, which are discarded after the launch.

WORKING DOGS

Written and illustrated by Stephen Roberts

Since Man first tamed wild dogs hundreds of thousands of years ago, he has bred, reared and trained them to do special jobs – guiding the blind; tracking and tackling criminals; herding sheep; finding missing persons; guarding homes and factories and pulling men over snow and ice. They have even followed soldiers into battle and been rocketed into space.

Police dogs

Throughout the world police forces use dogs to find missing persons, track down and sometimes tackle criminals, sniff out hidden drugs and explosives and control riotous crowds. A lot of hard work, time and patience goes into their training. One handler looks after a dog throughout its working life and the dog must obey every word of his command.

Sheep dogs

Throughout the world farmers use dogs to protect and control flocks of sheep. They are trained to round up sheep, to drive them carefully into pens, single out an individual sheep or find lost ones. A handler may work with one, two or sometimes three dogs, controlling them with special calls and whistles.

Guide dogs

There's a special relationship between a blind person and their dog. Through the special harness the dog can guide the handler through noisy, busy streets, across roads and on and off buses. Their training is very strict and great care is taken to ensure that the owner and the dog are well suited.

Gun dogs

People who shoot gamebirds or wildfowl for a living or for sport need a good gun dog to help them. Gun dogs are used to find and disturb the birds into flight for their masters to shoot. The dogs then retrieve the birds when they have fallen. Sometimes the birds fall into water so the dogs have to swim to bring them back.

Sledge dogs

For centuries people of the Northern Arctic regions, like the Eskimos, have depended on such dogs as the 'Husky' to pull sledges with them and their equipment across great areas of snow and ice. Many early expeditions to the polar regions could not have survived without using these dogs.

Fascinating Facts from Nature

Written and illustrated by Peter Harrison

The farmer's plough turns up all kinds of grubs and insects on which SEAGULLS feed, thus getting rid of some crop pests.

WOODPECKERS use their powerful beaks to drill out nesting holes and to get insects from the bark. A woodpecker drums on dead trees to let other woodpeckers know that he is in residence in his territory.

SWIFTS feed, mate and even sleep on the wing. They build their nests in the eaves of buildings or in crevices. If forced onto the ground they find it difficult to walk.

Birds have bills of different shapes because each species needs different food.
For example:

(top)	The HERRING GULL has a strong, hooked beak for tearing fish.
(middle)	The OYSTER CATCHER has a long, strong beak to probe and open shellfish.
(bottom)	ROCK PIPPETS have delicate beaks to catch insects.

With the start of spring LAPWINGS put on incredible flying displays. The male lapwing is trying to attract a mate.

The expression "as mad as a March hare" derives from the antics of the JACK HARE in springtime when he kicks, grunts, bucks and has boxing matches with his rivals.

The very rare LARGE BLUE BUTTERFLY lays its eggs on wild thyme. The caterpillar first feeds on the plant, but then develops a gland which produces a honey which is attractive to ants. Ants then carry the caterpillar into their nest, where the caterpillar feeds on ant larvae, while the ants eat the caterpillar's honey, until it is time for it to emerge as a butterfly.

The PRIMROSE and other woodland plants can flower only in the spring. Once the trees are in full leaf, the woodland floor is in perpetual shade and it is too dark for them.

Did you know that there can be as many as 7.2 *million* EARTHWORMS in one hectare of old pasture?

The SUNDEW (right) is a plant found in boggy land. It traps and digests insects, seeds and pollen to supplement the food it gets through its roots.

Did you know that the SEA ANEMONE is really a jelly-like animal which catches its food with its flower-like tentacles?

MOLES dig tunnels and patrol them to eat any creatures which fall in. Their main diet is earthworms and grubs.

Along the seashore look out for DOGFISH and SKATE eggs (mermaid's purses) which have been anchored to the seabed with long threads from each corner.

POND SKATERS are small insects which move about on the surface of the water. They can do this because of the effect of water tension whereby the surface acts like an elastic skin.

On the RIGHT TRACK

written and photographed by Michael Edwards

THERE IS a certain magic about model railways. I do not know whether this is due to the shiny, painted engines and carriages, perfect in every detail, or whether it's created by the realistic scenery.

Many of you will have your own model railway layout and you probably add to it from time to time. The photographs on these pages give you an idea of what a good model railway can look like when time, care and effort are put into it. Of course, it helps if Dad or an uncle is interested, too!

Here, everything is balanced and properly designed, with the scenery constructed at the early stages and not added as an afterthought. Even the ballast is of the correct size.

This layout represents a rural county branch line in the 1930s and is railway modelling at its best. Many of the buildings in this model actually exist. The splendid row of shops with a policeman standing on the corner is an exact replica of a scene in Cheshire. The model is so authentic that, when part of the original building collapsed, architects consulted the model to enable them to reconstruct every detail in the real building as before.

If you are interested in this fascinating hobby, why don't you join your local Model Railway Society. The members will put you on the right track from the start.

This is a garden scene near the marshalling yard, complete with greenhouse, hedges and wall.

Four hundred hours' work went into making this row of shops in Cheshire. Five hundred and fifty slates were individually made. However the shops are not just empty shells. Peep through the butcher's window and you will see scales, knives, and even meat on the slab. The MG car driver is wearing plus fours. The old style road signs and the correct costume all keep the setting in perfect period.

To obtain the life-like cement rendering and stucco finish of the Heybridge farmhouse, ordinary yellow sand was stuck onto the walls with glue and textured.

Notice the sagging guttering on the barn and milking parlour which is often seen but rarely modelled. The hay in the barn loft is rubberised horsehair painted straw colour.

This is the farm in the imaginary village of Heybridge. The red bricks of the outbuildings are computer punchings painted in the appropriate colour. There are 4,000 bricks and each one was stuck on individually.

The 'stone' viaduct looks totally authentic. It was constructed by fixing two plastic viaduct kits together. A splendid Steam Rail Motor, which took one year to build and which is now worth over £180, is crossing the viaduct. The running water effect of the stream under the viaduct was achieved by applying eleven coats of varnish. The layers gradually built up, and after about nine coats the stones and reeds were added. Two further coats bound it all together.

Fraddon Halt – a scene which conjures up memories of the age of steam as an old 2-4-0 locomotive puffs across the iron bridge.

A scene at the cattle market.

The realistic back scenes like this one looking across the coal yard are carefully painted and superimposed with photographs cut from calendars. This may seem easy, but in all the cut-outs the shadows in any one scene must all fall in the same direction. It is such attention to detail which separates the ordinary railway modeller from the enthusiast.

COLLECTING PICTURE POSTCARDS

Written and illustrated by Stephen Roberts

Let us imagine you are now reading the back of an old picture postcard. The postmark tells us it was posted on 9th August 1909, from Brighton, a popular seaside town on the south coast of England. The stamp of Edward the Seventh, who reigned from 1901 to 1910, shows us that it cost only one *old* halfpenny to send. We can easily guess that it was sent by a holiday-maker or day-tripper.

We call the early years of this century 'Edwardian' and it was during this time that picture postcards became very popular. Lots of people sent them and many collected them. Some received hundreds of cards all the year round; then placed them proudly into albums to show off to visitors.

Just like most people today, the Edwardians liked to send view cards of their home town or the seaside resort at which they were staying, to friends and relations.

Comic postcards were very popular. Many showed people at the seaside – riding donkeys, paddling, swimming and boating. Others made fun of the fashion, transport and inventions of the time such as telephones or motor cars and aircraft.

To please the collectors, the people who made postcards came up with all sorts of ideas. Postcards were used to send Christmas or birthday greetings. Some cards had small gramophone records stuck on to them and played *Happy Birthday* or Christmas carols. Feathers, ribbons, felt, tinsel and lace were all stuck onto the cards for decoration.

Picture postcards were still popular during the First World War. Soldiers sent cards home to their families. Some cards contained the words to popular songs of the day like *It's a long way to Tipperary*. Others had flags and flowers made of lace and silk.

Today you can buy all sorts of postcards. Many organisations produce their own cards – there are no prizes for correctly identifying the person on the right!

POST CARD

There are still many old postcards waiting to be discovered. Grandparents, aunts and uncles may even have some old postcards tucked away somewhere, which they received or collected when they were young.

Here you see the back of a modern picture postcard. This one too was sent from Brighton. It is still a popular seaside town and, like any seaside town, postcards are as much a part of holidays as candy-floss, rock or fish and chips.

A lot of people collect old picture postcards as a hobby or keep a scrapbook of postcards they buy as a record of places they have visited. In museums, art galleries or historic buildings you can find many interesting cards – aircraft, motor cars, animals, birds, works of art.

Why don't you start a collection of your own? Some photograph albums will hold postcards or you can convert any book into an album by making tiny slits in the page under which you slide the corners of the postcard. You can even keep them in old shoe boxes and arrange them under different subject headings.

ROCK ON

Written and photographed by Michael Edwards

How do the letters get into a stick of holiday rock? I didn't know, and nor did anyone else I asked. So, on behalf of *The Cub Scout Annual* I decided to find out. Arrangements were made for five Cub Scouts from the Leyland St. Mary's Pack in Lancashire to spend a day at the Fylde Coast Confectionery factory in Blackpool.

Holiday rock needs to be made at sea level due to the effect that altitude has on the water. With fifteen of the twenty-two manufacturers located in Blackpool, there are more rock makers in this famous resort than anywhere else in Britain, and Fylde Coast Confectionery is the second largest.

Mr. Douglas Loynds, the Managing Director of Fylde Coast Confectionery, met us at the entrance to the factory which makes 30,000 sticks of rock a day – that's almost 8 million sticks each year! As soon as we entered the building the distinctive aroma of rock filled our nostrils. Mr. Loynds took the boys on a guided tour of the factory. He told the boys that the basic ingredients of rock are granulated sugar, glucose, water and flavouring (like peppermint). One hundred and forty pounds of rock are made at one time: 84 lbs. of sugar, 56 lbs. of glucose, and 5 oz. of peppermint are dissolved in one gallon of water and boiled to 280°F. The mixture must be boiled correctly so that it will be crunchy (which is the sign of good rock) and not chewy.

The rock is then poured bubbling and seething onto warm metal trays. One tenth is taken for the casing and a further two per cent for the letters and red colouring added. The rest of the mixture (called a 'boiling' in the trade) is placed on a pulling machine which pulls air through it to make it lighter. The air bubbles transform the clear liquid into an opaque white substance. It's still warm and soft but, surprisingly, not at all sticky.

Mr. Garry Brooks and Mr. Paul Pilsbury pour the 'boiling' onto the cooling plates. Pink colouring will be added to part of the batch for the letters and the outer casing.

Miles McKenna and Edward Canning watch the pulling machine in action with Mr. Douglas Loynds.

Andrew Chester and Edward try their hand at kneading the soft white mixture after it has left the pulling machine. The Cubs discovered that even though the rock mixture was very soft, it wasn't sticky.

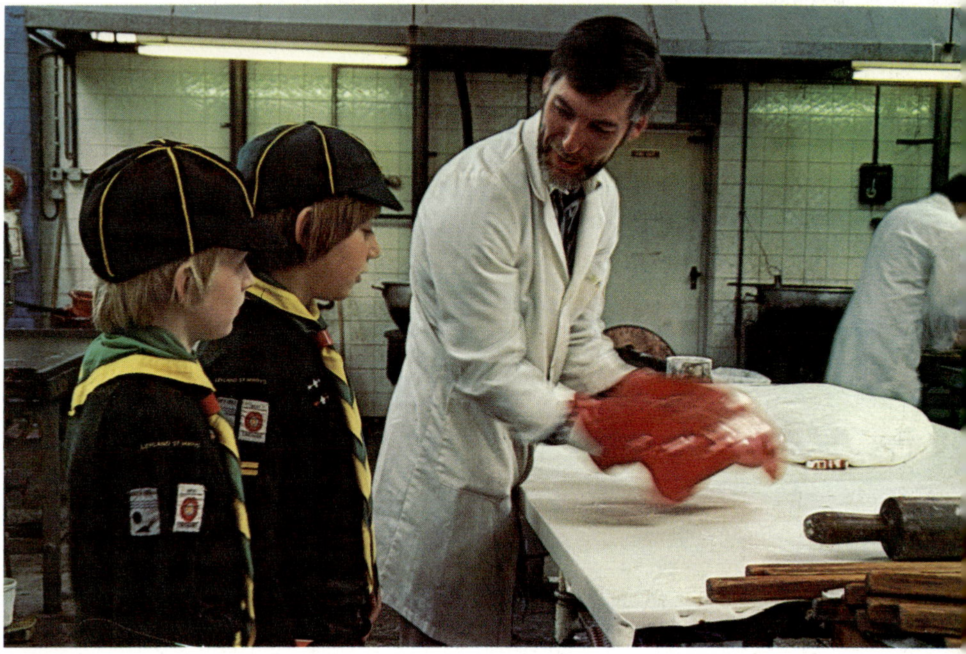

Mr. Douglas Loynds telling Miles and Gary Walmsley that the soft, red mixture he is holding will be used for making the letters and the outer casing, and this particular batch will have a peppermint flavour.

Mr. Geoff Nichol shows Miles and Edward how each letter is stretched to several feet and supported by teak wood splints to prevent the warm rock from going flat.

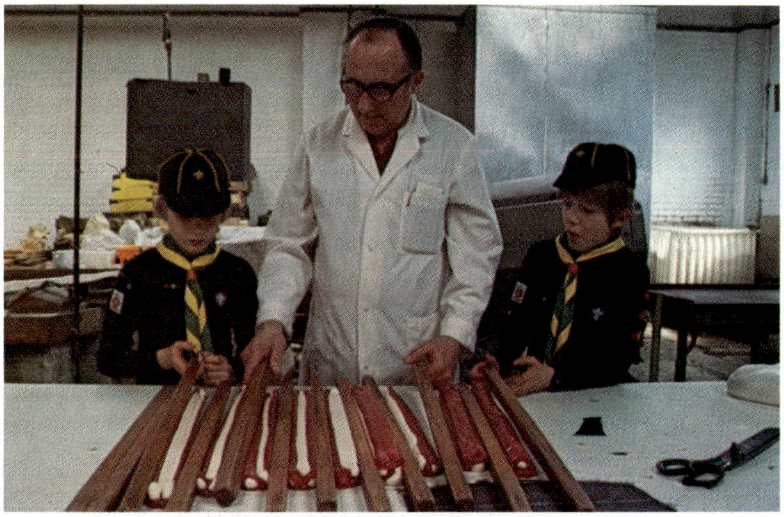

The most interesting and complicated process comes next – making the letters. The swiftness of the letterer's fingers deceives the eye. He makes it look so easy as he rolls and pats the soft red or white mixtures into the individual characters.

Most letters are too complicated for the beginner to tackle, but the letters 'O' and 'C' are relatively easy to make. For the 'O' a piece of white is rolled into a round stick. A lump of red is rolled until it is three inches wide and is then wrapped round the white.

As each letter is made it is placed between wooden splints to stop it going flat. The letters are built up from the centre and the red casing is rolled out and wrapped around the bomb-shaped lump of soft white rock containing those magical letters.

Any bubbles in the casing are popped with scissor blades so that no white patches will show on the finished rock. The soft rock lump is put into the revolving batch roller which draws the mixture to a point. A man called a spinner pulls out the end of the rock into a continuous length almost forty feet long. Now, for the first time, the mixture begins to look like holiday rock.

Further down the table several ladies roll the rock into its smooth, round shape and cut it into appropriate lengths. The sticks are left to cool and harden and are then wrapped in cellophane with a small photo label of the resort placed in the centre. Finally the sticks are packed in cartons ready for despatch.

Mr. Loynds' factory makes little 'Blackpool' rock. Most of his rock goes to Devon, Cornwall, Northumbria, East Anglia, Sussex and South Wales. The firm also supplies Warwick Castle, Longleat House and Blenheim Palace . . . and many batches are exported to several countries overseas.

Mr. Paul Pilsbury and Mr. Alen Taylor roll the 'boiling' before it is put into the batch roller.

Andrew and Adam Waterhouse watch the soft rock as it comes off the batch roller.

Adam, Andrew, Edward, Miles and Gary roll the uncut lengths into the familiar smooth, round shape of seaside rock.

When the rock has cooled and set hard it is cut. A gauge ensures that each piece is the same length. Here Andrew and Miles help Mrs. Lesley Miller lift the cooled sticks from the rolling slab before they are wrapped.

Mrs. Wendy Middleton and Mrs. Margaret Wharton show the Cubs how to wrap the individual sticks of rock, first putting a small photograph of the resort inside.

To make them round, the lollipops are put into a ball saw. Helped by the Cubs, Mr. Stephen Singleton and Mrs. Andrea Foley then insert the sticks.

Andrew, Gary and Miles watch as Mr. Tony Stayte cuts a length of rock for lollipops.

Fylde Coast Confectionery also make Kendal Mint Cake. Here, Mrs. Margaret Wharton shows Adam and Andrew how to break the slabs of Mint Cake into individual pieces before the sweet is packed into plastic bags.

THE CUB SCOUT ANNUAL *gratefully acknowledges the help and assistance of Fylde Coast Confectionery, and Mr. Douglas Loynds in particular, in the preparation of this feature.*

A Typical Cub Scout?

Is there a typical Cub Scout? We asked four of our artists to draw what they thought was a typical Cub Scout and you can see the results here! Each one is very different.

Just for fun, you can show us what *you* think a typical Cub Scout looks like. He can be amusing or serious; a drawing, painting or cartoon; in colour or black and white. It's up to you. There's an entry form with a space for you to do your drawing on page 61. We'll look at all your efforts, and send the 10 best entries a free copy of the 1986 Cub Scout Annual.

drawn by Peter Harrison

drawn by Leslie Cecil

drawn by Bill Bruce

Cliff Brown's Puzzle Page

YOU WILL FIND MORE OF CLIFF BROWN'S PUZZLES ON PAGES 6-24-57. ANSWERS ON PAGE 63

HOW WELL DO YOU KNOW YOUR PROFICIENCY BADGES?

THESE CUB SCOUTS AND THEIR MUMS ARE GETTING READY FOR A JUMBLE SALE TO RAISE MONEY FOR THEIR PACK. HIDDEN IN THE PICTURE ARE THE SYMBOLS FROM THE 25 PROFICIENCY BADGES.

CAN YOU FIND AND CORRECTLY NAME ALL OF THEM?

FOUR SPORTS WORDS

EACH BOX BELOW CONTAINS A SPORTY WORD OR WORDS TOTALLING NINE LETTERS. THE LETTERS ARE SET OUT SO THEY CAN BE READ BY STARTING AT ONE LETTER THEN MOVING TO THE NEXT VERTICALLY, HORIZONTALLY OR DIAGONALLY. WHAT ARE THE FOUR SPORTS?

1.

I	E	Y
E	C	K
H	O	C

2.

N	O	T
A	D	N
B	M	I

3.

S	E	L
C	T	H
I	T	A

4.

T	A	W
E	R	P
O	L	O

NOW TRY AND SEE HOW MANY WORDS OF THREE OR MORE LETTERS YOU CAN GET FROM EACH SQUARE, USING THE SAME RULES, FOR EXAMPLE, TO GIVE YOU A START ON SQUARE 4 —

WART, PAW, RAT, RATE, POLE...

ANOTHER SPORTING ACTIVITY

JOIN THE DOTS IN NUMERICAL ORDER TO DISCOVER WHAT IT IS.

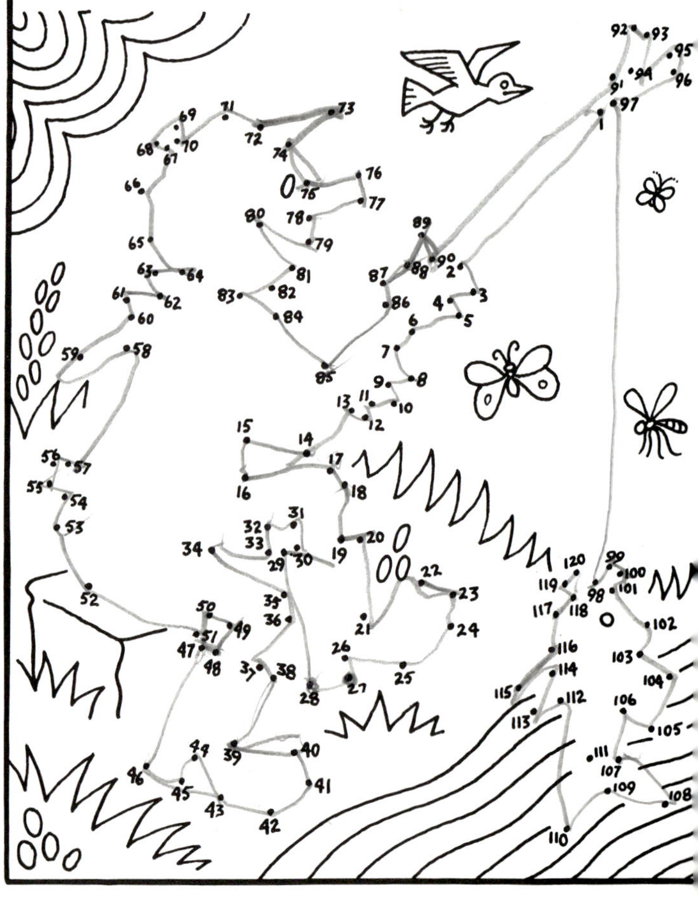

THE FRUIT CROSSWORD

by Nancy Scott

Clues Across:

3. The first fruit mentioned in the Bible (5)
5. All fruit is attached to a ---- (4)
7. Jack put in his thumb and pulled out a ---- (4)
8. A citrus fruit with a reddish-yellow rind (6)
9. All fruit looks pleasing to the --- (3)
12. A ---- fruit is one that is not common (4)
13. A small, soft fruit that makes delicious jam or jelly (9)
15. The sun causes fruit to ----- (5)
17. These are often eaten with cream (7)
19. When fruit is cooked with an equal quantity of sugar it is called --- (3)
20. This is put over fruit bushes to keep out birds (3)
21. These need to drop before the fruit forms (6)
23. An insect which pollenates a fruit tree's flowers (3)
24. A fresh plum should have a lovely ----- on it (5)
25. These come from a palm tree (5)

Clues Down:

1. A precious stone or the brand name of some fruit sweets (4)
2. Another fruit often eaten with cream, but this one grows on the ground (10)
4. Citrus fruits that make a refreshing drink (5)
6. These are dark red stone-fruits (8)
7. These sound as though they're joined together in twos, but the spelling is different (5)
10. The colour of grass and what sounds like a measuring instrument make up the name of this fruit (9)
11. You may receive a bunch of these if you are ill (6)
14. Insects --- the nectar in the fruit blossoms (3)
16. These grow in large yellow "hands" (7)
18. This fruit cuts into large juicy sections (5)
22. Every fruit grows from a ---- (4)

Solution on page 63

LET'S GO EXPLORING

By Jack Cox and Bill Bruce
Illustrated by Bill Bruce

Have you ever imagined yourself to be like one of the great explorers – Columbus, Drake, Cook, Livingstone or Amundsen? You cannot hope to dash off around the world as they did – but you can be an explorer without going too far from home.

Every Cub Scout makes a natural explorer – he wants to know just how to find out all the answers . . .

Every large, untidy garden is a challenge; every woodland path or winding stream has its secrets to tell and by exploring you'll soon discover them.

Your own doorstep . . .

What better place to start than around your own home. Do you know when your house was built? Who lived there before you? If it's a new house, do you know what the land was used for before building began? You can look for the answers to these questions by asking local people or by looking at old maps and plans in your local library or council offices.

What is the name of the street where you live? Is it named after a famous local person and, if so, who was he and what did he do?

Go into the garden and start to explore . . . you may think you already know the garden well, but you could be wrong – there are always new things to find.

A broken air brick at the base of the chimney could be just large enough to allow a garden toad to spend the winter in the warm. There may be an old house martin's nest under the eaves: does a wren or other small bird live there in the winter?

Is there a drain cover somewhere at the edge of the lawn? Where do the drain pipes go from there? Find a thin cane and by poking through the ground trace the drain's course – perhaps the pipes re-appear outside the garden or dive down deep to go under a wall.

Do you know what's on the other side of your garden wall or fence? When did you last look?

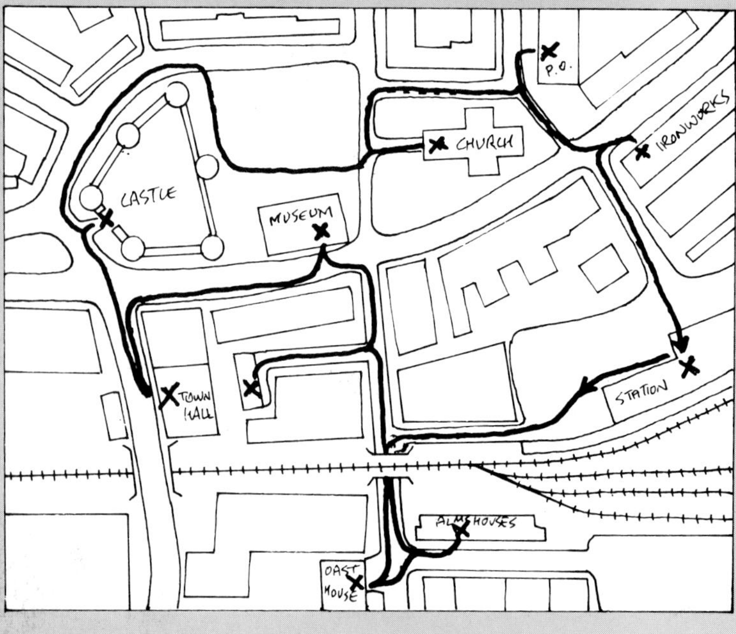

When you go exploring you will be able to see much more if you plan your route carefully before you go. In case you make a mistake in your planning, and so you don't damage the map, put a piece of clear plastic over it and mark your route on that using a suitable felt tip pen or a chinagraph pencil. When working out a possible route use your map-reading skills to spot problems along the way. You don't want to climb too many steep hills nor to cross a river where there is no bridge! Try to plan your route so that you do not go to the same place twice, but don't be too ambitious – it is better to go to the same place twice than to try to cram too much into one day.

So that your map does not get damaged, and so that you do not have to open and close it every time you need to look at it, make a map board. Take a piece of hardboard, make two holes at the top and thread through a piece of strong cord: this will enable you to hang the map board round your neck, leaving both hands free. Attach your map and a sheet of clear plastic to the board with a bulldog clip. Your map board is finished and you are ready to start exploring.

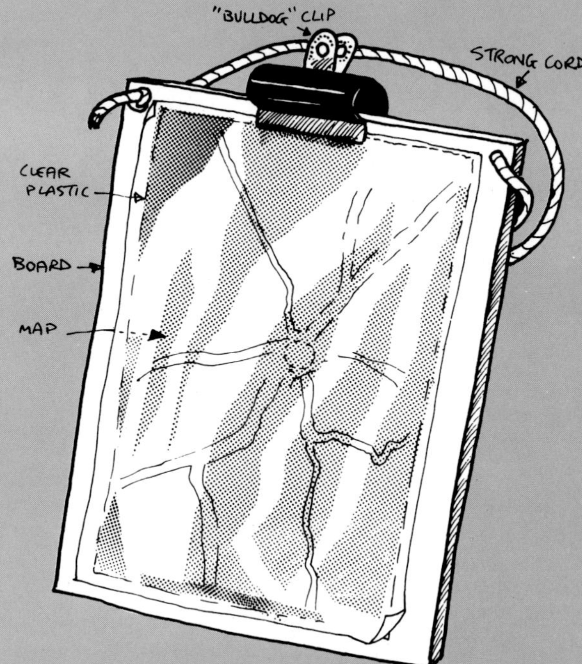

As an extra record of your trip it's a good idea to make your own map of the area you have explored, noting all the major buildings and features. Mark a route on it, and see whether your friends can follow it: if they can, you have made a good map.

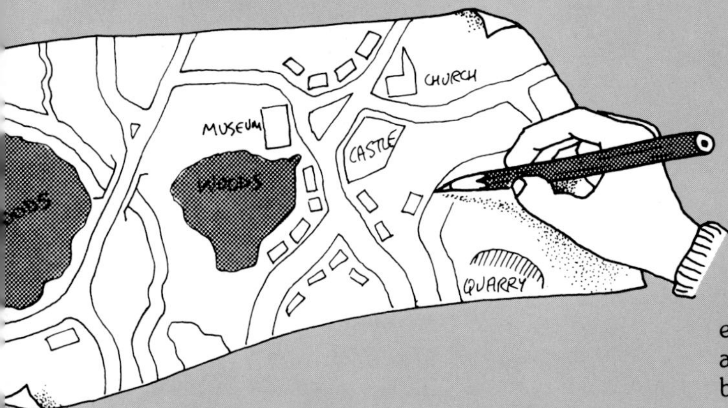

Around the town and in the country . . .

Do you know the history of the place where you live? You can find out quite a lot by going out and exploring.

Old plaques and statues can tell you much about the people and events of the past. Many buildings bear the date in which they were built. A pillar box always carries the initials of the monarch in whose reign it was made.

Local churches can tell you more than most other places about the past. There are so many different types of church building, and nearly all are open to the public for at least a part of the day. Headstones and tombs in the churchyard outside will give you a selection of the townspeople of the past, and brass or stone plaques inside may tell you even more. Why not make some brass rubbings as souvenirs of your exploration? (But remember to ask permission first.)

Do you know where all the footpaths and alleys in the town lead to? Never trespass on private property, and always try to remember where you are and how you got there. Take a notebook and pencil with you to make notes about your route and anything interesting you discover along the way. So that you don't get lost, put down tracking signs as you go . . . as they are to help you on the return journey, set them in reverse! Let an adult know where you are going.

The local public library is the richest source of the young explorer's information with books and maps going back for perhaps hundreds of years. A good explorer is always well prepared and finds out as much as possible before he starts out. The more you know before you begin, the more you'll enjoy the expedition.

Make plenty of detailed notes about your explorations so you can compare them with the information you get from people or the library. If you have a camera take some photographs and/or make some sketches. You could organise a Pack competition to see who can discover the most information about the town, the school, or a place of local interest.

Exploring in safety

Don't be tempted to go too far on your own. The experienced explorers always travel in teams, and anyway it's more fun to go in a group. It is also much safer because if one of you becomes ill or has an accident, there is someone else to go for help.

Always tell someone (e.g. your parents or Cub Scout Leaders) where you are going, how long you expect to be and the route you expect to take. If you are delayed, do your best to telephone, so that the people back home do not become worried by your late return.

Keep to footpaths when travelling along roads, but if there is no path, always walk in single file, facing the oncoming traffic, and wear bright clothes so that you can be seen easily.

If you are going out for the whole day, you will need to take a number of things with you. You'll want food and drink, your map board, a compass, notebook and pencils and possibly a guide book covering the area you are going to explore. Don't forget to take some money in case you need to make an urgent telephone call, and always carry some form of identification. Pack your gear in a rucsac or small day-sac on your back. Take more things than you think you might need: a good explorer, like a good Cub Scout, is always prepared.

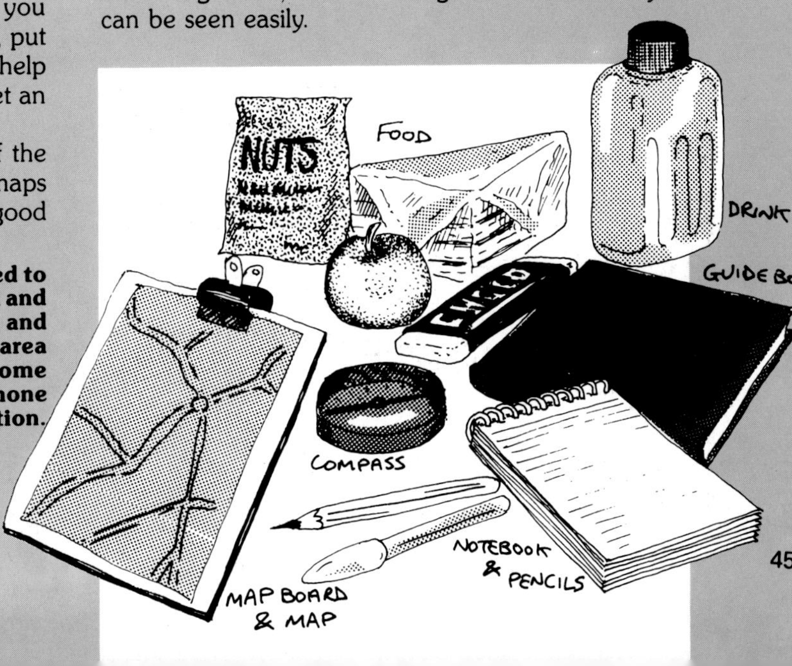

You could use tracking signs to help you find the way back over a difficult part of the route but remember to lay the signs backwards to show you the way back. There are many tracking signs but these are the main ones you'll need.

A. This way – straight on

B. Turn left (or right)

C. Not this way

If you are walking as a group, gauge your speed by that of the slowest member of the team – or one of you is sure to be left behind! Always follow the *Highway Code* and the *Country Code.* Make sure you get home before it gets dark because you're much more likely to lose your way in the dark.

Check the local weather forecast before you start out. Be prepared for a change in the weather. If you know the weather's likely to be rough, put off your trip – you can always explore on another day.

Keep away from railway lines and river banks. Don't go too near old canals and drainage ditches.

If you have to cross water, find a bridge – there is no sense in getting your feet wet. Keep away from old and derelict buildings and machinery, which are full of such hazards as rotten stairs, broken glass and rusty metal. A sensible explorer never knowingly puts himself in danger.

Always carry a card with your name, address and telephone number, some food (if you'll be out for more than an hour or so) and some money for a telephone call. If you do get lost, don't waste time trying to find your own way home – ask someone for directions.

Wear sensible clothes for your explorations. Take into account any possible changes in the weather. Carry a waterproof jacket in case it rains and an extra sweater in case it becomes cold. You'll enjoy yourself more if you keep warm and dry.

Finally, a good explorer is never afraid to say: "I'm tired – let's go home now . . ."

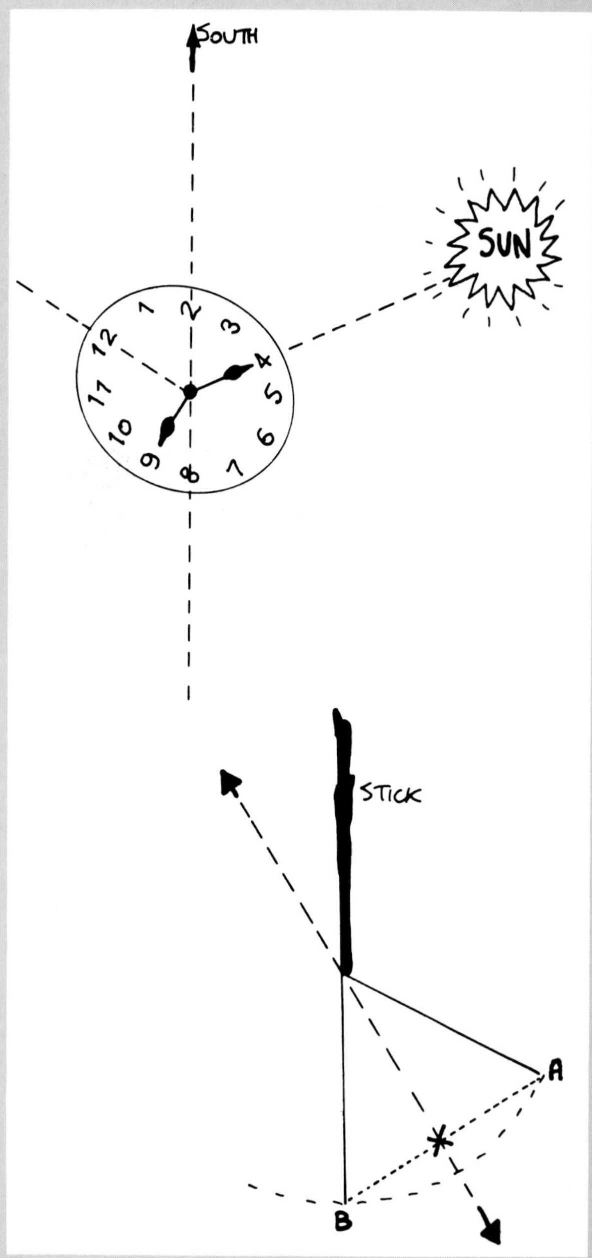

If you do become lost, DO NOT PANIC! Even the most experienced explorers lose their way from time to time. Ask for help and try to use your map and compass. Whether or not you are lost, as an explorer you should be able to find north and south without a compass . . .

top **Point the hour hand of your watch towards the sun and SOUTH will be in approximately the direction midway between the hour hand and 12. If it is summer you will first need to put your watch back one hour so that it is in Greenwich Mean Time.**

bottom **If you do not have a watch (but have some time!) you can find the NORTH-SOUTH line by pushing a stick into the ground about two hours before noon. Note the position of the end of the stick's shadow (the longer the stick, the more accurate this will be). Tie a length of string at the base of the stick and lie the string along the shadow. Fix it at the point where the shadow ends (A). Swing the string in an arc along the direction of the shadow's movement on the ground. At noon the shadow will have shortened, and then it will grow longer. Mark the point where the shadow meets the arc again (B). A line joining the base of the stick and the mid-point between (A) and (B) will be the NORTH-SOUTH LINE.**

Some Cub Scout Puzzlewords

by Suzanne Brown

1. Clues

1. There is a chess piece on this badge (7)
2. The Grand ---- is performed at Pack Meetings (4)
3. A Cub Scout promises to do his best "to keep the Cub ----- ---." (5, 3)
4. A Scout uses his ---- hand for the Scout Handshake (4)
5. Found on the Sportsman Proficiency Badge (8)
6. (*across*) Scouting was started by ------ Baden-Powell (6)
6. (*down*) A meeting of many Cub Scouts (5)
7. A Cub Scout does a Good ---- every day (4)
8. A ------ helps a Sixer (6)
9. The ---- Help badge is a Proficiency Badge (4)
10. One of the Arrow Badges (6)
11. A Cub Scout may work for the ---- Reader Badge (4)

Clues

1. In which month was Baden-Powell born? (8)
2. Cub Scouts ----- for their Badges (5)
3. These games are played outside (9)
4. A Cub Scout learns to follow tracking signs for this Arrow Badge (6)
5. (*across*) The Scout Motto (2, 8)
5. (*down*) The Union Flag is unfurled at the Flag ----- ceremony (5)
6. A group of Scouts (6)
7. Scouts have a special --- week when they try to earn money for their Scout Group (3)
8. A Proficiency Badge (11)
9. The Cub Scout Salute is made with ----- fingers (5)
10. The background colour of single stage Proficiency Badges is --- (3)
11. At his Investiture Ceremony a Cub Scout is presented with his ----- Scout Badge (5)

3. Clues

1. Cub Scouts may work on -------- (8)
2. In 1907 a camp was held on -------- Island (8)
3. A ----- may be used in First Aid (5)
4. Baden-Powell was a Major- ------- in the British Army (7)
5. A Cub Scout who wishes to become a Scout works for his ---- Badge (4)
6. Found on the Photographer Proficiency Badge (6)
7. There is a -------- on the Naturalist Proficiency Badge (8)
8. May be made of wood (5)
9. A compass has ----- cardinal points (5)
10. A type of game (4)
11. --- Scouts may travel in canoes or dinghies (3)

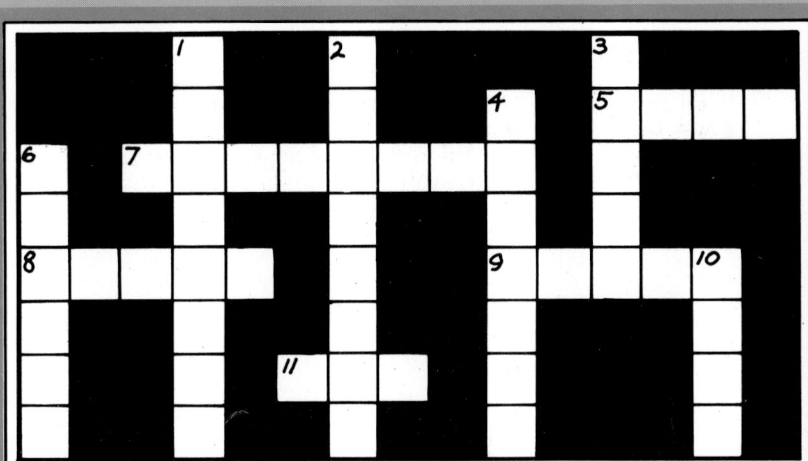

Solutions on page 63

Collecting Scout Stamps

by Walfredo Bellioni

When you were young, how many of you spent hours on a beach collecting all sorts, shapes, colours and sizes of pebbles or rocks or shells? How often did your mother turn out your pockets and find buttons, bits of wood, stones and all sorts of other things? Quite often, I expect. These were the first signs of your instinct to collect things.

When you were a little older perhaps you started to collect other items like leaves which you mounted on card, or different badges, stickers, programmes or key rings. Whatever you collected you'll have had fun arranging them, and perhaps labelling each one and adding some of your own notes.

I wonder how many of you collect stamps, and in particular those which are associated with our great Scout family. Well, it's never too late to start! There are Scouts in over 120 countries, many of which have issued stamps showing Scout activities and pictures of Lord and Lady Baden-Powell.

Philately (the correct name for stamp collecting) with a Scouting theme started with those stamps issued by the Cape of Good Hope (the southernmost tip of Africa) in 1900 at the time of the Boer War. They were produced by makeshift means – one shows a picture of Robert Baden-Powell, and another a cadet sergeant cyclist. Why do these stamps mark the beginning of Scout philately when Scouts didn't even exist in 1900? At that time Baden-Powell was the commanding officer of the garrison defending the town of Mafeking which was beseiged by the Boers. Baden-Powell used boys from the town as cadets to help the military. He was impressed by the way in which the boys responded to the responsibility placed on them.

The first real Scout stamps were issued in 1918 by Czechoslovakia which, during its struggle for independence, used Scouts to deliver the mail. The stamps were overprinted 'Posta Ceskych Scautu'. In 1920 Siam (now called Thailand) overprinted some stamps showing the head of a tiger and gave a part of the revenue from their sale to Siamese Scouts.

In 1925 Hungary issued the first stamp showing an actual picture of a Scout. In 1933 Hungary issued a series of stamps to commemorate the 4th World Scout Jamboree which was held in their country. Between 1931 and 1936 Rumania issued five series of stamps with a Scouting theme. From then on numerous countries issued stamps to honour our world-wide Brotherhood.

Today, hundreds of stamps with a Scouting theme are issued by the most distant countries of the five continents – from the Solomon Islands in the Pacific to St. Kitts in the Caribbean, from Benin to Iceland, from Mexico to Nepal . . . and so on.

By collecting stamps you will discover something about the countries in which there are Cub Scouts belonging to the same great Scout family as yourself. You'll learn that the currency in India is the *rupee*, in Rumania the *lei*, on the island of Tonga the *paanga*, and in Japan the *yen*. A whole new world will be opened up for you! Philately will give you the chance to write to Cubs in other countries to swap your spare stamps. If you're a good businessman you'll find that your collection increases in value over the years, while you have the enjoyment of adding more stamps to it year by year.

The Scout Stamp Collectors Club

by Peter Duck

The SCOUT STAMPS COLLECTORS CLUB was founded in 1957 following the increased interest in Scout stamps aroused by the numerous stamp issues commemorating the Centenary of Baden-Powell's birth and the Golden Jubilee of Scouting.

Club membership is now over 700 people world-wide and extends to collectors of Scout and Guide stamps, Postal History of Scout and Guide events, Special Postmarks, Slogans and Meter Cancellations, Labels and Postcards.

Cub Scouts can join as individual members for £1.50 a year, or a Pack may become a group member for £2.50 a year. Applications or enquiries should be sent to:

Mr. R. D. Lee, Membership Secretary,
The Scout Stamps Collectors Club,
57 The Jordans, Allesley Park,
COVENTRY CV6 9JS

The world's leading collectors who specialise in Scout and Guide stamps belong to the Scout Stamps Collectors Club, and their expert advice and knowledge is available to fellow members.

A Bulletin is published six times a year. It give details of New Issues of stamps and postmarks, and articles on events of philatelic interest. There are also announcements of Postal Auctions and Sales Services, and advertisements of members' and dealers' sales and wants. A Junior Section was started in 1982.

Regional Meetings are held where members can meet for special displays and to exchange news and items for their collections.

New Issue Services supply mint stamps, First Day Covers, special covers, etc. at the lowest prices.

As you may remember 1982 was 'The Year of the Scout' when Scouting celebrated its 75th Birthday. All round the world countries issued stamps to commemorate the occasion. You can see some of the miniatures on this page, and a small selection of other stamps on the next two pages.

SCOUT STAMPS

THE YEAR OF THE SCOUT 1982

stamps collected by Peter Duck

design and layout by Malcolm Turner

1st ASCENSION SCOUT GROUP
The Year of the Scout
1907~1982
ASCENSION
10p
15p
25p
40p
ZAMBIA
ZAMBIA SCOUTS 1907·1982
K1
The GAMBIA
75th ANNIVERSARY OF SCOUTING
85b
Turks & Caicos Islands
75th Anniversary of Scouting
75c
SEA SCOUT CRICKET MATCH
75e ANNIVERSAIRE DES BOY-SCOUTS
REPUBLIQUE TOGOLAISE
90F
REPUBLIQUE CENTRAFRICAINE
300F
75e anniversaire du scoutisme
75th Anniversary of Scouting
1907–1982
NIGERIA
THE FRIENDLY ISLES
TONGA
75th Anniversary of Scouting
REPUBLIQUE FEDERALE ISLAMIQUE DES COMORES
75F
75e anniversaire du scoutisme
NAURU
40c
GRENADA GRENADINES
$3.00
125th ANNIVERSARY · BIRTH OF LORD BADEN-POWELL
ANIMAL TENDING
125th ANNIVERSARY · BIRTH OF LORD BADEN POWELL
GRENADA
70c
75e anniversaire du scoutisme
14UM
POSTES
REPUBLIQUE ISLAMIQUE de MAURITANIE
75th Anniversary of World Scouting
HELPING DISABLED
KENYA
5/-
SUMMER ISLES
SCOTLAND
20P
PARAGUAY
75 ANIVERSARIO DE LA FUNDACION DE LOS SCOUTS
Gs.10
PILIPINAS
P200
75th Anniversary of the SCOUT MOVEMENT
45c
FIJI
20p
75th ANNIVERSARY · BOY SCOUT MOVEMENT
GHANA
75th Anniversary of Scouting 1907·1982
B-P's Last Message
BE PREPARED
STICK TO YOUR SCOUT PROMISE ALWAYS!
ISLE OF MAN
24p
MAURITIUS
R10
Transkei
25c
15t
Papua New Guinea

1982 The Year of the Scout on Stamps

How the Royal Mail works today

Today our postal service is far removed from the messengers and mail coaches of olden times.

It has to be! Every day the Royal Mail handles 38 million letters and parcels – and at Christmas the daily total reaches 100 million.

That enormous amount of mail requires a vast, smooth running operation to handle it, especially when you think that the Post Office aims to deliver 90% of first class letter mail on the next working day after collection, and 96% of second class letter mail by the third working day after collection.

Here's an example of how a letter would get from Bristol to London today:

1. A letter is posted in the afternoon.
2. A postman comes later in the afternoon and empties the contents of the posting box into a mail bag.

3. When the van arrives at the local Sorting Office the mail bag is loaded onto a chain conveyor which takes the letter to the sorting machinery.
4. The mail bags are emptied into a machine called a segregator which separates letters from packets. Another machine, the automatic letter facer, or 'ALF', then segregates first from second class, puts on the postmark and turns all the letters round the correct way.

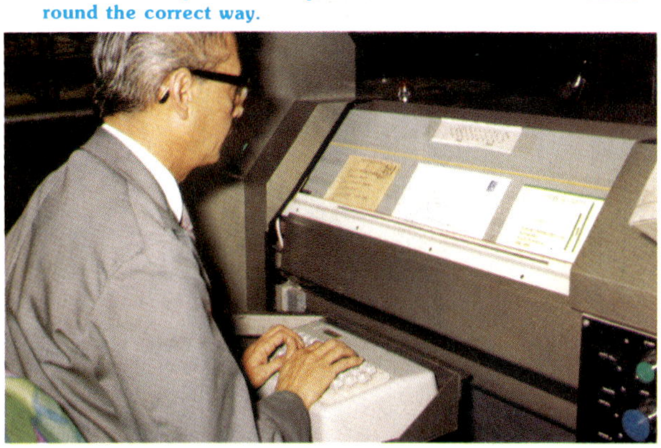

5. Letters then go to the coding desks where the man at the keyboard reads the postcode on each envelope and instructs the machine to put phosphor dots on each letter. These dots are the postcodes in 'machine language'.

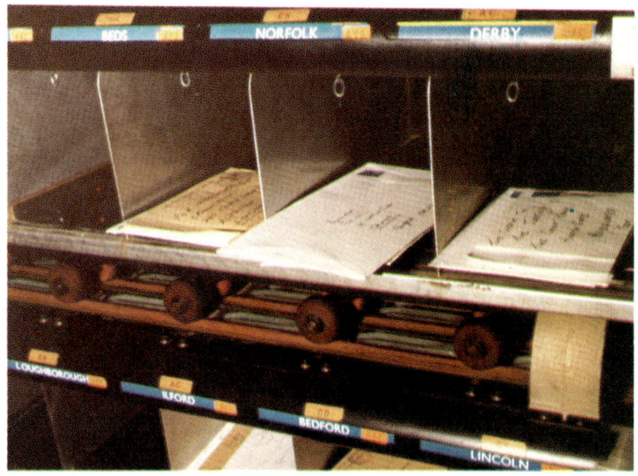

6. The sorting machines, which are linked to a computer, can read the phosphor dots – which tell them the letters' destinations – and the letters travel along belts and are dropped into the correct box for each destination.

7. A mailbag for our letter's destination in London is made up and taken from the Sorting Office to the train to London.
8. The mail is unloaded at Paddington station less than two hours later.
9. At the London Sorting Office the sorting machinery reads the phosphor dots on the envelopes so it can sort the letters for each postman.
10. The postman can then go out and deliver his letters.

TRAVELLING POST OFFICES

Because so much sorting of letters has to be done in such a short time it is sometimes done on board the trains taking the letters to their destinations.

These trains are called travelling post offices. A travelling post office operates at night from London to Bristol and postmen sort the letters during the journey. This is much faster than the old mail coaches!

THINGS TO DO

The Post Office has a wealth of interesting history – and today's stamps become tomorrow's collectors' items.

If you want to start a stamp collection – or if you already have one but would like to learn more – why not join the Stamp Bug Club?

Six times a year you will receive a copy of Stamp Bug News, keeping you up to date with British Stamps. There are competitions, crosswords, swaps and news.

Ask at your post office for information or write to Stamp Bug Club, Freepost, PO Box 109, Baker Street, HIGH WYCOMBE, Bucks HP11 2TD.

Coaches were in use years before John Palmer's scheme to use them for carrying mail was introduced.

Why not start a scrap book and fill it with as many pictures of old coaches as you can find? Look through magazines – or see if local museums have postcards.

We gratefully acknowledge the co-operation of the Post Office, South Western Postal Region, which prepared this feature especially for THE CUB SCOUT ANNUAL. *Illustrations and photographs © Copyright the Post Office.*

The AMERICAN COWBOY

by Frank Humphris

The history of the American cowboy is a long one. It began in Mexico following the conquest of that country by Cortes and his small army of conquistadores (*con-kees-ta-dor-es*) in 1519. The Spaniards brought the first cattle to Mexico and during the next three centuries they gradually spread north with their herds of cattle and mustang horses, and established settlements and ranches in the south western part of what is now the United States. A vast area which included the present states of Texas, Arizona, New Mexico, Nevada and California, belonged then to Mexico. The ranches employed men to handle the cattle, and these men, mostly of mixed Spanish and Indian blood, were known as 'vaqueros' from the Spanish word 'vaca', meaning cow.

When the Anglo-Americans from the eastern states moved west and settled in Texas in the early 1800s, they adopted the same working methods in handling cattle as the Mexicans.

They also used the same equipment, as we shall see.

As the herds grew they were allowed to graze on the open plains without fences. The climate and conditions suited the cattle and their numbers rapidly increased. The technique of ranching was now developed, with seasonal round-ups when the calves were branded with their owners' marks.

The use of the rope, lariat or lasso also developed during this period, enabling the animals to be caught when necessary. The animals themselves, living as they did in wild open country, grew hardy, long legged and wild, and developed very long horns, hence the term, 'longhorns'. It was their descendants that formed the great herds that went up the trails from Texas, during the heyday of the cowboy.

In 1836, the Anglo-Americans — now numbering several thousands — rose against the Mexican government and after defeating a Mexican army declared Texas a republic. Following the fighting, many Mexicans fled back to Mexico leaving their cattle on the open ranges. These were now taken over by the American — we should now call them Texan — ranchers and cowboys.

Naturally, over the 300 years that passed since the conquest of Mexico the dress of the vaqueros changed considerably. In early times a rough cotton shirt and trousers worn under the ever-useful poncho, or blanket, was the usual gear — bare feet were quite common among the poorer herdsmen, spurs being worn round the bare ankle. Conditions were very rough and primitive. But as time passed the Mexican vaquero would look something like the illustration. A wide-brimmed sombrero protected his head, and a short jacket, sometimes trimmed with braid, would be worn with tight flared trousers. Over the trousers were a pair of close fitting leather leggings. He was a superb horseman, an expert with the lariat and all work connected with the range.

A MEXICAN VAQUERO

THE WESTERN SADDLE is essentially a working saddle. The early frontiersmen and cowboys bought their saddles from the Mexicans. The Mexican saddle had developed from the mediaeval saddles brought over by the conquistadores and was designed for the type of riding and work done by the vaqueros. It had a high pommel with a saddle horn for use when roping, wide stirrup leathers with large box stirrups and a single cincha (Spanish for girth) located at the front. This type of rig is typical of the Mexican and early Californian saddles. Many carried large saddle bags, or cantinas, at the rear, and the large horn, looking like half a grapefruit, is still popular today.

MEXICAN SADDLE

The Texan cowboy adopted the Mexican saddle but gradually altered it to suit his own ideas. The large horn was replaced by a smaller, iron one, the seat was improved and a second, or flank cinch, was added. Over the years the shape of the pommel, or forks as the cowboys call it, was widened to form a grip for the rider's legs. For bronc riders they were deeply undercut to give a particularly good grip. Gradually the features were refined as conditions on the ranches changed, but there are still many styles available to suit different riders.

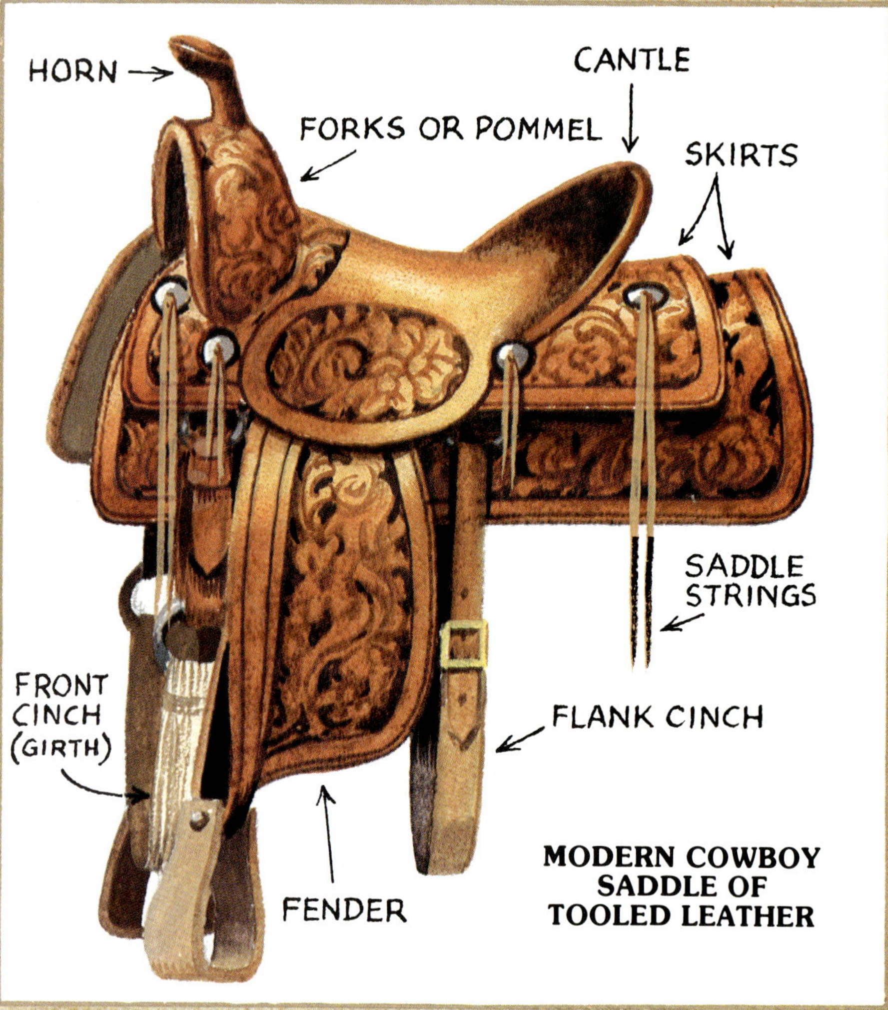

MODERN COWBOY SADDLE OF TOOLED LEATHER

SPURS
The spurs worn by the cowboy look rather large and menacing, but, in fact, the points of the rowels are quite blunt. In the days when the cowboy's mount was a half-wild mustang, they were necessary to get obedience in a difficult and often highly dangerous job.

TAPADEROS (TAPS)
Many saddles were fitted with stirrup covers, or hoods, to protect the rider's feet from thorns, cactus and rocks when riding in rough country. There were many styles, some were plain and simple, others were decorative with embossed leather to match the saddle.

LARIAT
The word is from the Spanish, 'la reata', meaning 'the rope'. The word 'lasso', ('lazo Spanish) means a snare, or noose, and is rarely used by the cowboy. The Mexican reatas were made from twisted or plaited rawhide, but the modern cowboy uses ropes of manilla or hemp — or even nylon.

ROWEL

SPUR STRAP

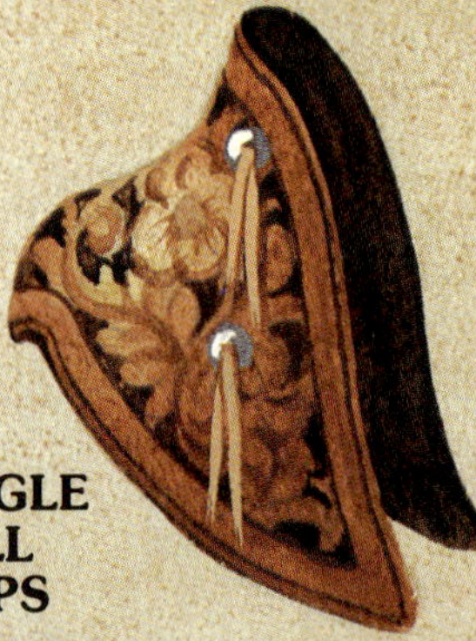

EAGLE BILL TAPS

BULLDOG TAPS

RAWHIDE LARIAT

'CHAPS' is the American term for the heavy leather leggings worn by cowboys. The word comes from the Spanish 'chaparejos', sometimes spelt 'chapareras' and they have a long history going right back to old Spain. They are worn to protect the legs from the thorns and heavy brush and when working among cattle.

Each leg is separate, being laced together in front with a leather thong and fastened behind the waist with a buckled belt. There are three main types, the most popular at the present time being the 'batwing' style. Each leg is formed of a large piece of leather – often three feet wide – which is folded round the leg and clipped together, leaving a 'wing' or flap at the side. The conches on the outside show where the clips are fastened. Even with this type there are three styles: the California style has five clips, the Texas style has four clips and the Cheyenne style has three clips.

The closed leg style – usually called shotgun chaps as the two legs resemble the twin barrels of a shotgun – were popular in the old days. The Mexicans mostly wore this style with tight legs fastened with leather loops and buttons. Sometimes they were fastened with buckles. The American shotgun style is usually sewn or laced at the sides and often decorated with a fringe or conchos.

Angora goatskin was, and is, the most practical of the fur chaps, or 'woollies'. In the damper and colder climate of the northern ranges and in the high foothills of the Rockies, the thick hair will be better in rain than leather chaps, which tend to become stiff and uncomfortable. In the early days bearskin chaps were quite common. The thick hair chaps give protection from bruises and scrapes when riding broncs.

On the American frontier it was necessary for men to go armed for self protection. In the early days there were wild Indians, outlaws and rustlers, and it was up to the individual to protect himself and his property until law and order was finally established. Men carried revolvers, either in their pockets or in open-topped holsters. The early six-shooters were percussion muzzle loaders, sometimes known as 'cap and ball' guns, for those were the days before metallic cartridges. Then, in 1873, the Colt company brought out the six-shot, Single Action Army Model, firing a .45 calibre metallic cartridge. This rapidly became the most popular revolver on the frontier and was the official side-arm of the U.S. cavalry. It was a favourite with the cowboys, for its robust and simple construction made it ideal for carrying in all weathers.

This is the gun you see used in most western films, though it is worth remembering that the wild gun fights shown are mainly a figment of the film maker's imagination.

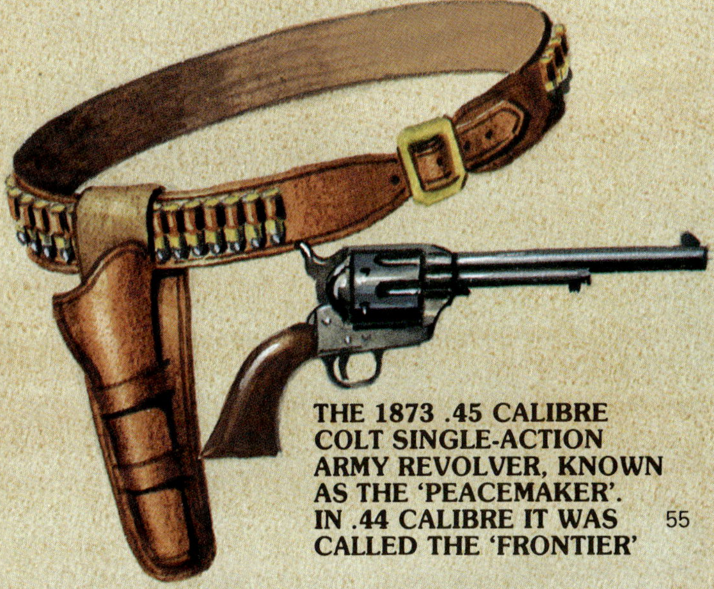

THE 1873 .45 CALIBRE COLT SINGLE-ACTION ARMY REVOLVER, KNOWN AS THE 'PEACEMAKER'. IN .44 CALIBRE IT WAS CALLED THE 'FRONTIER'

TRAIL HERD IN THE 1870s

Texas had the cattle — a thousand miles to the north were large industrial cities that needed the beef. The great cattle drives to these vast new markets began in earnest after the end of the Civil War in 1865.

The most famous route became known as the Chisholm Trail and led from Texas to the railroad town of Abilene in Kansas. Further west, the Western trail led to Dodge City which became known as the cowboy capital.

The average herd numbered about 2,500 and to drive this there would be the trail boss, from eight to twelve cowboys, a cook and the horse 'wrangler', the man who looked after the horse herd, for each cowboy had five or six horses in his 'string'. It was hard, dusty, monotonous and often dangerous, for the trail crossed Indian country, semi-desert regions, and rivers where the cattle had to be forced to swim.

The men were up before sunrise and were in the saddle by dawn, urging the cattle on and keeping them from straying. Meals were taken at the chuck wagon, which was constructed with a sort of larder at the back, in which the food for the journey was kept. The food itself was monotonous, being mostly bacon and beans with a few changes depending on the skill of the cook with what was available.

COWBOYS HAVING A MEAL AT THE CHUCKWAGON AT THE END OF A LONG DAY'S DRIVE.

The horse ridden by the cowboy was a descendant of the Spanish horses brought over by the conquistadores and those who followed. They were generally small and tough and, being bred on the open ranges, were wild. They were called mustangs — another Spanish word. Being used to running free on the range, they had to be 'broken', or gentled, before they were any use as a saddle horse or cow pony, and this was the job of the bronco-buster. 'Bronco' is Spanish for a rough, unbroken horse.

The horse was first roped, then there was a struggle while the cowboy put on a halter and saddle. Once the rider was mounted the horse would rear and buck in a frenzied attempt to dislodge the 'thing' on its back. Bronco-busting was rough and dangerous work.

Cliff Brown's Puzzle Page

YOU WILL FIND MORE OF CLIFF BROWN'S PUZZLES ON PAGES 6–24–42.

ANSWERS ON PAGE 63

DAN'S GOOD DEED

DAN'S MUM HAD A BROKEN VASE, AND HE SAID HE WOULD MEND IT FOR HER. THE TROUBLE WAS THERE WERE EIGHT PIECES AND ONLY ONE WOULD FIT. WHICH PIECE DID DAN USE TO MAKE THE VASE WHOLE AGAIN?

FIND THE FAMOUS WRITER

THE PICTURES UNDER THE GRID ARE 'DOWN' CLUES. COMPLETE THE FOUR LETTER WORDS AND A FAMOUS WRITER'S NAME WILL APPEAR ON THE 'ACROSS' LINE BETWEEN THE ARROWS. WHO IS HE?

RHYMING PAIRS

ALL YOU HAVE TO DO IS TO PUT THE WORDS DESCRIBING THE TWENTY PICTURES BELOW INTO TEN SETS OF RHYMING PAIRS. TO GIVE YOU A START... 3 AND 5 (LINK AND WINK) NOW DO THE REST.

COMPETITION

This year's competition is sponsored by World International Publishing Limited (the official Annual publishers of The Scout Association).

THE PRIZES

FIRST PRIZE: A prize of the winner's choice up to £100 in value

SECOND PRIZE: A prize up to £50 in value

THIRD PRIZE: A prize up to £25 in value

25 RUNNER-UP PRIZES OF

The International Cub Scout Book **(value £4.50)**
and
The Outdoor Adventure Book **(value £2.50)**

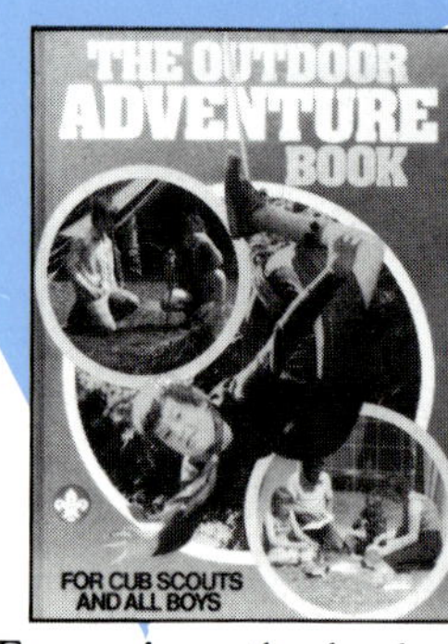

NAME THESE TUNES

This year we've got a competition with a difference! We're not only giving you an opportunity to show us your musical skills, but we're also asking you to tell us what prizes you would choose if yours was the first, second or third correct entry out of the sack.

You probably sing quite a lot – in school, in your place of worship, round the camp fire . . . maybe you have your own radio and join in or hum or whistle the latest pop songs. Some of you will be learning a musical instrument. Certainly it's most unlikely that a day will pass without your hearing music of some sort. Now, whether or not you can read music will be another matter. Anyway, we thought we'd let you show us how good (or bad!) you are at music *and* give you the chance to win a fabulous prize.

Here's what you have to do

1. On the page opposite you will find the opening bars of twelve well-known songs, carols or hymns. All you have to do is to tell us the title of each one. If you cannot read music, ask someone who can to play or hum the tunes to you.
2. On the Entry Form on page 61:
   a. write your answers clearly in BLOCK CAPITALS in the appropriate box.
   b. let us know what First Prize (value £100) you would choose and, in not more than 12 words, tell us why you would choose it; what Second Prize (value £50) you would choose; and what Third Prize (value £25) you would choose.
   c. fill in your name, address, date of birth and Cub Scout Pack.
   d. let us know which *three* items you most enjoyed in this Annual.
   e. give *two* suggestions for features you would like to see in future Cub Scout Annuals.
3. Carefully cut out the Entry Form along the broken lines and send it, to arrive not later than 31st January 1984, to:
   1984 Cub Scout Annual Competition,
   Editorial Department, The Scout Association,
   Baden-Powell House, Queen's Gate, LONDON
   SW7 5JS

The Rules

1. All competitors must be under the age of 11 years on 31st December 1983.
2. The closing date for the competition is Tuesday, 31st January, 1984.
3. All the correct entries will be placed in a sack. The FIRST PRIZE will be awarded to the first complete, correct entry drawn at a date to be arranged in February 1984. The SECOND PRIZE will be awarded to the second complete, correct entry drawn, and so on.
4. Prize winners will be notified by post, and the full list of winners will be published in SCOUTING Magazine.
5. While every effort will be made to provide each winner with the prize of his choice, both The Scout Association and World International Publishing Limited reserve the right to substitute an alternative prize.
6. The Editor's decision is final. No correspondence can be entered into, and entries cannot be returned.

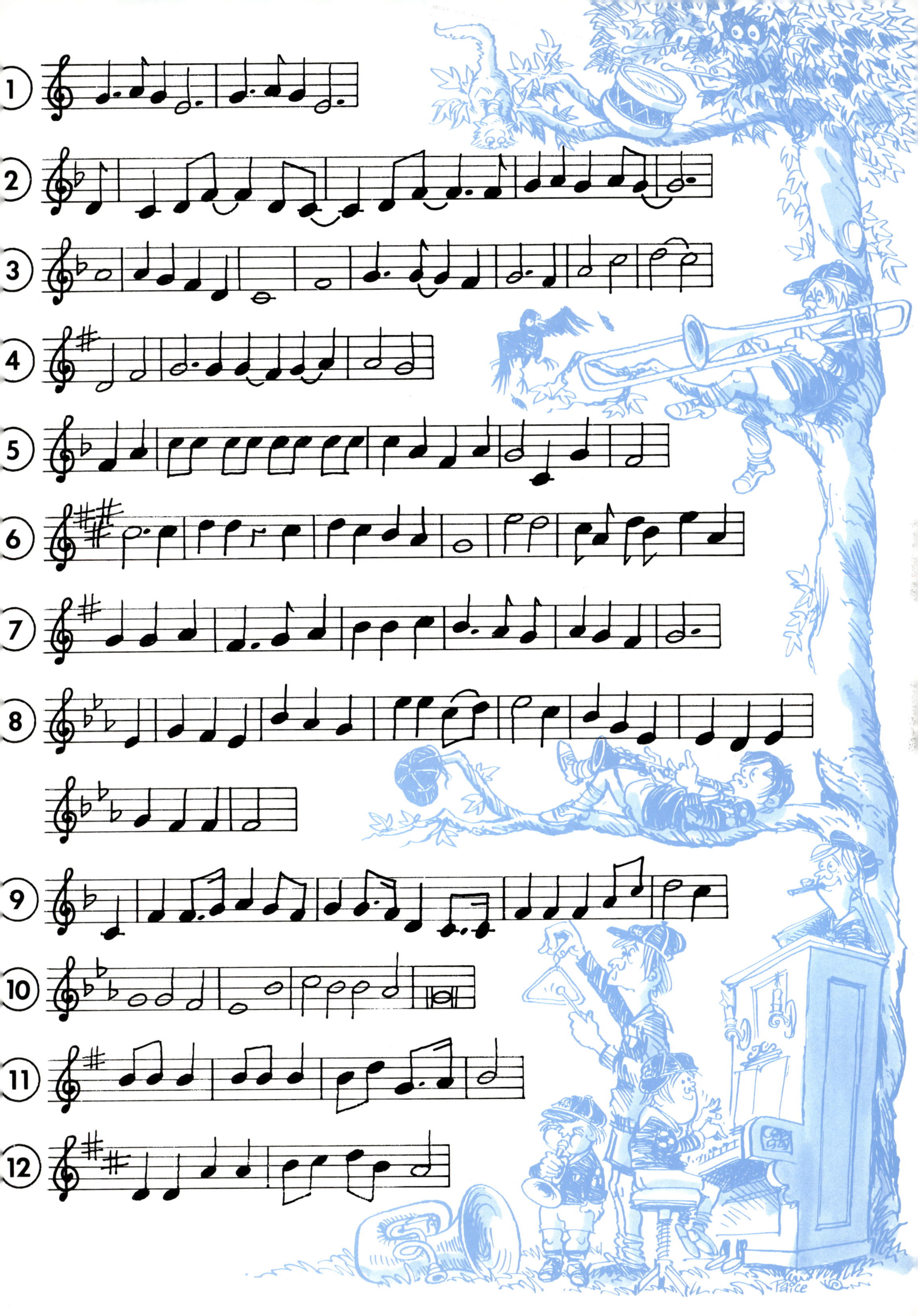
1
2
3
4
5
6
7
8
9
10
11
12

GIFT-WRAPPED

by Eric Franklin

In recent years a new phrase, "gift-wrapped", has come into common use. It means simply that, instead of a gift just being perhaps wrapped up in brown paper and tied with string, the gift is more carefully wrapped in decorative paper and tied with something more exotic, such as brightly coloured ribbon. Since today gift-wrapping has become almost commonplace, I thought we could go one better and offer our small gifts in an ingenious little puzzle box which could give the recipient some fun in addition to the pleasure of the gift. I mention small gifts since this little puzzle box cannot practically be made much larger than, say, 4″×4″×2″ (100×100×50 mm).

The best material with which to make the box is a sheet of thick cartridge paper and this can be obtained in various colours from art shops. To make a box of the dimensions mentioned above you will need a piece 12″ square (300 mm): smaller boxes for trinkets such as brooches, necklaces, etc., could be made from squares of 10″ (250 mm), 8″ (200 mm) or, for really small gifts, even 6″ (150 mm).

With a pencil and ruler divide the sides into four equal parts and lightly draw the connecting lines shown by the thin lines in Fig. 1. Then draw the diagonal lines as indicated. With a heavier pencil thicken the lines which are shown with a thick line in the illustration. Now, with sharp scissors (or, better still, a modelling knife) first cut away the eight shaded triangular pieces. Then cut into the sheet along the thick black lines. The two slots can only really be cut with a knife and these should be made with two cuts about one millimetre apart and the little slice carefully removed. The slots in the other two corners should leave a sort of tongue the same width as the slots. (Ask an adult for help with this.)

You now have to make up the box and it will help if you lightly score along all the thin lines with the back of your knife or with a steel knitting needle. Fig. 2 shows the box half folded and Fig. 3 the completed box. To get the tongue through the slot, fold in the corners but *do not crease them* and, with a little patience, you will get them through, smoothing out the tongue afterwards.

If you have made your box from brightly coloured paper, this may be enough, but you may want something more striking. Why not make the box from metal-foil-backed paper which can be bought in quite brilliant colours? Alternatively, you could decorate the box with your own drawings, with transfers, or with cut-outs from magazines or perhaps a gardening catalogue. Another idea is to use a thinner paper and paste it onto a piece of brightly coloured wallpaper. If you like, you could tie up the box with a fairly wide ribbon to disguise the flaps and then have fun while you watch them puzzle out how to open the box and get at their gift.

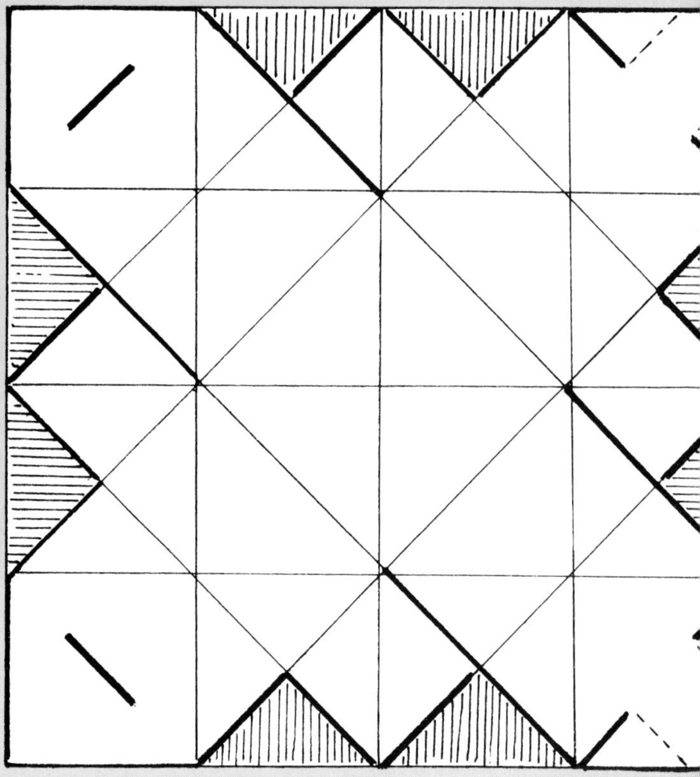

Fig.1.

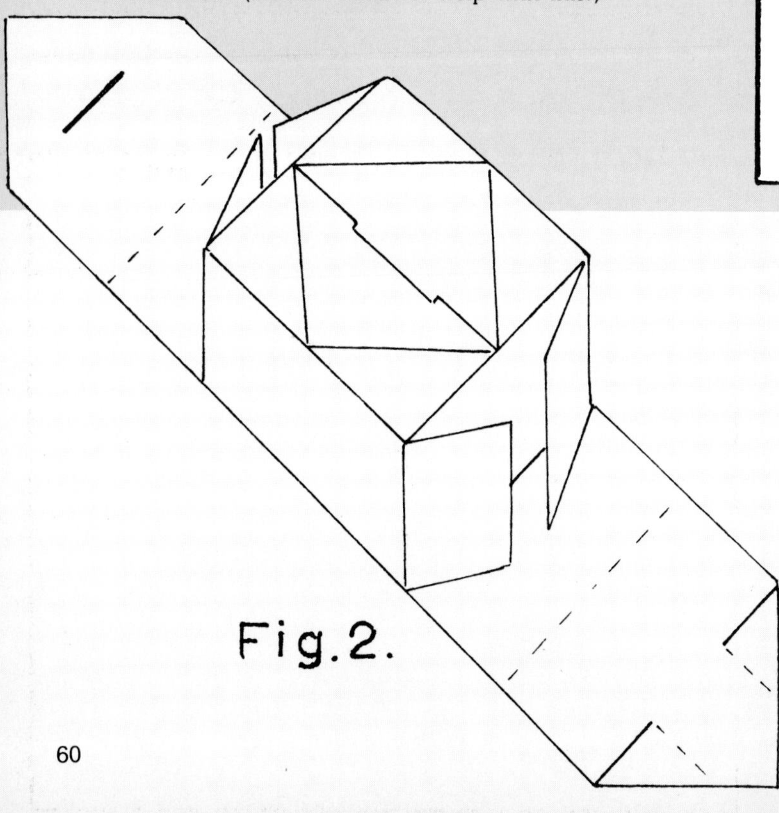

Fig.2.

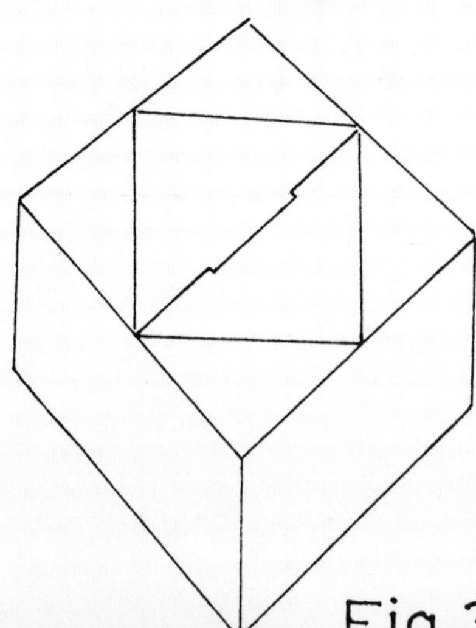

Fig.3.

Name These Tunes Competition Entry Form

: 1984 Cub Scout Annual Compeition,
Editorial Department, Baden-Powell House,
Queen's Gate, LONDON SW7 5JS.

.EASE COMPLETE THIS FORM IN BLOCK CAPITALS

AME ______

DDRESS ______

______

______

JB SCOUT PACK ______

______

ATE OF BIRTH ______

won First Prize (up to £100 value) I would like ______

______

ecause (not more than 12 words): ______

______

______

I won Second Prize (up to £50 value) I would like ______

______

I won Third Prize (up to £25 value) I would like ______

______

e three items I most enjoyed in this Annual were:

______

______

______

would like to make these suggestions for
atures in future Cub Scout Annuals:

______

______

CLOSING DATE 31st. JANUARY 1984

ANSWERS

1. ______
2. ______
3. ______
4. ______
5. ______
6. ______
7. ______
8. ______
9. ______
10. ______
11. ______
12. ______

cut carefully along this line

A Typical Cub Scout

(see page 41)

o: 1984 Cub Scout Annual, Editorial Department,
Baden-Powell House, Queen's Gate, LONDON SW7 5JS.

AME ______

DDRESS ______

______

______

UB SCOUT PACK ______

______

______

ATE OF BIRTH ______

Draw your typical Cub Scout here

THE 1985 CUB SCOUT ANNUAL Presents

INSIDE THE COVERS OF THE **1985 CUB SCOUT ANNUAL** YOU'LL FIND ALL SORTS OF GOOD THINGS. EACH FEATURE HAS BEEN ESPECIALLY PREPARED FOR YOU. ON THE TREE YOU'LL FIND JUST A FEW OF THE PRESENTS WE'LL BE GIVING YOU.

THE 1985 CUB SCOUT ANNUAL IS A '**MUST**' FOR EVERY CUB SCOUT SO... ORDER YOUR OWN COPY EARLY **OR** MAKE SURE IT'S AT THE TOP OF YOUR 1984 CHRISTMAS LIST.